INTERPRETING THE PARABLES

A. M. HUNTER

Interpreting the Parables

SCM PRESS LTD

334 00685 6

First published 1960
by SCM Press Ltd
58 Bloomsbury Street, London WC1
Revised edition 1964
Eighth impression 1981
Printed in Great Britain by
Richard Clay (The Chaucer Press) Ltd
Bungay, Suffolk

CONTENTS

PREFACE

THIS BOOK attempts to show the ordinary reader, in some hundred pages, how modern scholars understand the parables of Jesus. How much it owes to C. H. Dodd and J. Jeremias[1] a glance at the Authors' Index will reveal. But I have not always agreed with them.

The book also tries to do two things more: (1) to sketch the history of interpretation from apostolic times until today, and (2) to suggest how parables, originally addressed to a specific historical situation in Palestine 1,900 years ago, can still speak to Christians in the twentieth century. Here I try to answer two questions which confront every preacher: (a) Is all *allegorizing* of the parables forbidden? (b) How far are we entitled to *moralize* them?

Scriptural passages are in nearly every case taken from the *Revised Standard Version of the Bible*.

My cordial thanks are due to my friend the Rev. Mitchell Hughes, Librarian of Christ's College, who helped me with the proofs.

A. M. HUNTER

Aberdeen
April 1960

[1] References to J. Jeremias, *The Parables of Jesus* have been changed to correspond to the revised edition of the book, published in 1963.

1

INTRODUCING THE PARABLES

THE IMPORTANCE of our subject may be gauged by the fact that the parables of Jesus comprise roughly one-third of his recorded teaching. Its popularity commands no better witness than that of the little girl who, being asked what bits of the Bible pleased her most, declared her preference for 'the like sayings'. And certainly, with the exception of the Lord's Prayer and the Beatitudes, no part of his teaching is better known or loved. Not a day passes but we quote the parables, often unconsciously. We talk about 'acting the Good Samaritan' or 'passing by on the other side'. Some of us 'bear the burden and heat of the day'; others indulge in 'riotous living'. Some use their 'talents' rightly; others 'hide their lamp under a bushel'; and others leave things to 'the eleventh hour'. We 'count the cost', or we 'pay the last farthing'. All these everyday phrases—and how many more—come to us from the parables.

Yet this verbal familiarity with them does not necessarily mean that we understand them rightly, or that we do not often make them teach lessons they were never designed to teach. It is easy to make fun, for example, of the early Fathers when we find Augustine identifying the Inn-keeper in the Good Samaritan with the apostle Paul, or Tertullian equating the fatted calf slain for the feast with the Saviour himself. But have we any right to criticize them if we find a warrant for *laissez faire* economics in The Labourers in the Vineyard or use The Tree and its Fruits as an argument for eugenics?[1]

[1] So Dean Inge, *Vale*, 76: 'Our Lord gives us some admirable eugenic principles', and he quotes, 'Do men gather grapes of thorns or figs of thistles?' But others have used The Tares as an argument against eugenics!

7

Interpretation, then, is going to be our main business in the following pages; but before we come to it, we must find answers to some basic questions.

1. What is a parable? In Sunday School we were taught to define it as 'an earthly story with a heavenly meaning'. For those starting Bible study this can hardly be bettered; but it is not precise enough for the pundits. If we wish to please them we had better define it as a comparison drawn from nature or daily life and designed to illuminate some spiritual truth, on the assumption that what is valid in one sphere is valid also in the other.

Parable is a form of teaching. 'Almost all teaching', Dean Inge has said,[1] 'consists in comparing the unknown with the known, the strange with the familiar'. It is a matter of everyday experience that you can hardly explain anything at all except by saying that it is like something else, something more familiar. So the Gospel parable often begins: 'The kingdom of God is like leaven . . . or a grain of mustard seed . . . or a dragnet'. (Notice, by the way, that you cannot stop there: you must follow the parable to the end if you are to discover the point of comparison. The Kingdom is not like leaven but like what happens when you put leaven into meal. And so on.) Combine, then, this mode of teaching by analogy with the Oriental's innate love of pictorial speech and everyman's delight in a story, and you have most of the reasons why men took to using parables to communicate truth. But who made the first parable, and how many centuries it was before Christ, are questions, as Sir Thomas Browne would say, 'above antiquarism'.

The word itself, *parabole*, is of course Greek, and means a comparison or analogy. Aristotle discusses it in his *Rhetoric*.[2] But the antecedents of Christ's parable must be sought not in Hellas but in Israel; not in the Greek orators but in the Old Testament prophets and the Jewish Fathers. Doubtless it was in the synagogue that Jesus first heard men talking in parables. But observe: the Oriental does not distinguish between a

[1] *The Gate of Life*, 73.   [2] *Rhetoric*, 2.20, 2 ff.

proverb and a parable; and the Hebrew word *mashal* (with its Aramaic equivalent *mathla*), derived from a verb meaning 'be like', is a pretty wide label for any verbal image, from a figurative saying (e.g. Ezekiel's 'Like mother, like daughter') or a proverb ('Is Saul also among the prophets?'), up to a proper parable (like Nathan's famous one about the ewe-lamb), an allegory (like Ezekiel's about the Eagles and the Vine) or even a long apocalyptic prediction (of which the 'parables' of Enoch are examples). When therefore the men who made the Greek Old Testament, the Septuagint, chose *parabole* to translate *mashal*, it attracted to itself most of *mashal's* meanings. And this is why in the New Testament, which owes so much to Septuagint usage, proverbs like 'Physician, heal thyself' and dark sayings like 'The things which come out of a man are what defile him' are called parables equally with long stories like The Talents.

In germ, then, a parable is a figurative saying: sometimes a simile ('Be wise as serpents'), sometimes a metaphor ('Beware of the leaven of the Pharisees'). What we call parables are simply expansions of these. 'All we like sheep have gone astray' is a simile. Expand it into a *picture* and you get a similitude like The Lost Sheep. Expand it into a *story* by using past tenses and circumstantial details, and you get a story-parable like The Prodigal Son. The difference between a similitude and a story-parable is this: whereas the similitude bases itself on some familiar truth or process (like putting a patch on a garment or leaven into meal), the story-parable describes not what men commonly do but what one man did. 'A sower went out to sow.' 'A certain man made a great supper.' If you want a rough grammatical test,[1] you may say that the first class — figurative sayings — have only one verb, the second class—similitudes—more than one verb, in the present tense, whereas the third class—story-parables—have a series of verbs, all in the past tense.)

All these are parables in the Biblical sense. They are not allegories. What is the difference?

[1] C. H. Dodd, *The Parables of the Kingdom*, 18.

Though, as we shall see, some of the Gospel parables have allegorical traits and one of them, The Wicked Vinedressers, can only be described as 'an allegorical parable', we must distinguish quite clearly between an allegory and a parable. The difference to remember is that in an allegory (like Addison's *Vision of Mirza* or Bunyan's *Pilgrim's Progress*) each detail of the story has its counterpart in the meaning, whereas in a parable (like The Lost Coin or The Friend at Midnight) story and meaning meet not at every point but at one central point. This point of likeness the pundits call the *tertium comparationis*. A parable usually has only one *tertium;* an allegory may have a dozen. In other words, the allegory is a kind of 'description in code', and, if it is to be fully understood, it must be deciphered point by point, feature by feature. On the other hand, in the parable there is one chief point of likeness between the story and the meaning, and the details simply help to make the story realistic and so serve the central thrust of the parable —like the feathers which wing the arrow.

The other difference to bear in mind is this: the true parable, if it is to fulfil its purpose, must be life-like—must hold the mirror up to life. By contrast, the allegory need not conform to the laws of life-likeness and probability and may stray off into some 'never never' world where eagles can plant vines and stars become bulls. In a parable things are what they profess to be: loaves are loaves, stones are stones, lamps are lamps. But in an allegory it is not so. The room which the woman sweeps in the parable of The Lost Coin is a room in any Galilean 'but-and-ben'; the room which the man sweeps in *The Pilgrim's Progress* is not a room but 'the Heart of a Man that was never sanctified by the sweet Grace of the Gospel'.[1]

2. We are ready now to ask: How many parables are there? (We are of course confining our attention to the Synoptic Gospels. It is commonly said that the Fourth Gospel contains no parables, only allegories. This is too sweeping a statement. The saying about The Woman in Travail (John 16.21) has a

[1] B. T. D. Smith, *The Parables of the Synoptic Gospels,* 22.

good claim to be called a parable. So has the Traveller at Sunset (John 12.35 f.); and an authentic parable of Jesus may be embedded in John 10.1-5.)[1]

A man's count will depend on how many of Jesus' short figurative sayings he includes in his reckoning. (Trench counted 30 parables; Bruce 33 plus 8 'parable germs'; Jülicher 53; and B. T. D. Smith finds 62.) Our own answer would be: 'about 60'.[2] Four of these, which teach not by analogy but by direct example (The Pharisee and the Publican, Dives and Lazarus, The Rich Fool, and The Good Samaritan) are usually called 'example stories'. The rest are either similitudes or story parables of the kind we have described. And one, the Last Judgment scene, often called the parable of The Sheep and the Goats, refuses to be classified.

Three features of the parables, which will concern us later, deserve brief mention here.

Consider them, first, as examples of popular story-telling. Down the long centuries men have found by experience that stories become more effective if you follow certain rough rules in telling them. Repetition in the 'build-up' of a story is a common one. Another is 'the rule of contrast' whereby virtue and vice, riches and poverty, wisdom and folly are set in sharp contrast. Yet another is 'the rule of three', whereby the story has three main characters ('An Englishman, an Irishman, and a Scotsman . . .'). A fourth is the 'rule of end stress' whereby the spotlight falls on the last in the series, whether it is the youngest son or the final adventure. Call them the storyteller's 'tricks of the trade' if you like; *raconteurs,* the world over, from time immemorial, have used them. Jesus employed them too. The tales of Dives and Lazarus and of The Wise and Foolish Virgins illustrate the rule of contrast. The three travellers in The Good Samaritan or the three excuse-makers in The Great Supper exemplify the rule of three. You may observe the rule of repetition in The Talents or The Two

---

[1] J. A. T. Robinson, *Zeitschrift für die Neutestamentliche Wissenschaft,* 46 Bd., 1955, 233-40.
[2] See list of parables (according to sources) at the end of the book.

Builders. The sending of the 'only son' to the Vineyard illustrates 'end stress'. A knowledge of these rules sometimes helps
us to the true interpretation of a parable. To take one example
only: there can be no doubt that in The Talents the stress
should fall on the end—that is, on the episode of the third
servant who hid his talent, so that it would be fair to say that
the two successful characters are only there in the story as foils
to this 'barren rascal'.

The second point to seize is that the Gospel parable is something extemporized in living encounter with men rather than
something lucubrated in study or cell. If the sonnet, for example, grows slowly in the soil of quiet—is essentially
'emotion recollected in tranquillity'—the parable is often im-
provised in the cut-and-thrust of conflict. For Jesus' parables,
as we shall see, arise out of real situations and are not seldom
instruments of controversy in which he justifies his actions,
vindicates the Gospel against its critics, or confronts men
with the clear and inescapable will and purpose of God. In
particular, the great parables which proclaim 'the wideness of
God's mercy' were *ripostes* extorted from him in his encoun-
ters with the Pharisees—'instruments forged for warfare and
the means whereby his strategy was vindicated—until no further words could serve—but only an Act'.[1]

The third point follows from this. Every parable of Jesus
was meant to evoke a response and to strike for a verdict.
'What do you think?' he sometimes begins, and where the
words are not found, the question is implied. There follows,
as a rule, a true-to-life story or the description of a familiar
happening; and the hearer is invited to transfer the judgment
formed on the happening or story to the urgent issues of the
Kingdom of God, which is the theme of all his parables. 'He
who has ears to hear,' he sometimes concludes, 'let him hear.'
Which must mean: 'This is more than just a pleasant story.
Go and work it out for yourselves.' Need we add that, since a
parable is often used to help home a disagreeable truth, it is
often spoken at some personal risk to the speaker? Nathan

[1] C. W. F. Smith, *The Jesus of the Parables*, 272.

put his own life in danger when he challenged an Oriental despot with his story about the ewe-lamb. Jotham told his parable of the Bramble to the men of Shechem, and then fled for his life. And in the greatest crisis of all, with the skies lowering and Calvary looming near, our Lord himself, in his tale of The Wicked Vinedressers, employed his own death-sentence as a weapon in his cause.

3. All we have been saying has paved the way for the question: Why did Jesus use parables?

The short answer is: to quicken understanding, by putting truth in a vivid and challenging and memorable way.[1] And therefore, if the notorious verses in Mark 4.11 f. mean what, at first glance, they appear to mean—that Jesus deliberately used parables to hide God's truth from the multitudes and make them ripe for judgment—they cannot be words of Jesus. (Our own view, briefly set forth in an appendix at the end of this book, is that they are genuine words of Jesus but that they do not belong here.)

For consider. Jesus knew himself to be God's Messenger to Israel at the supreme moment of her history, called to alert men to the great crisis which was the inauguration of the Reign of God. If his 'alarm signals' (and many of his parables were just that) were to work, they could not afford to be un-clear. As St Paul said (I Cor. 14.8): 'If the trumpet gives an indistinct sound, who will get ready for battle?' Accordingly, Jesus' parables, when first uttered, cannot have been dark riddles designed merely to mystify the multitudes.

Yet this conclusion must be held along with the recognition that the Gospel parable is not always sun-clear, and certainly must not be regarded as the ancient equivalent of an 'illustration' in a modern sermon—sugar-coating for the theological pill or a concrete example from life to make the truth memorable. The Gospel parable is designed to make people

---

[1] 'God tells the truth in parables,' said Abraham Lincoln, who was himself fond of using them, 'because they are easier for the common folk to understand and recollect.'
Adlai E. Stevenson, *The Observer*, Feb. 8, 1959.

think. It appeals to the intelligence through the imagination.
And sometimes, like the smoked glass we use to observe an
eclipse, it conceals in order to reveal. Seen thus, the parable
is not so much a crutch for limping intellects (as so many
'illustrations' are) as a spur to spiritual perception.[1]

One further observation. The parable, by its very nature, is
hard to contradict. Demanding an opinion on its own human
level (The Two Debtors is a good example), the parable finds
an opening which makes the hearer lower his guard and leaves
him defenceless. Then, before he is aware of it, the sword-
thrust is home: 'Thou art the man!' Or, as P. G. Wodehouse
makes one of his characters say: a parable is one of those
stories in the Bible which sounds at first like a pleasant yarn
but keeps something up its sleeve which pops up and leaves
you flat. But if the parable is hard to contradict, how much
also it can convey! What solemn warnings, what heart-search-
ing accusations! Yes, but also what gentle and gracious
assurances of God's mercy and God's love! (We might forget
a sermon on God's Fatherhood or a lecture on the Idea of
Grace, but who that heard it could forget Christ's story about
the father and his two sons?)

4. Where did Jesus get the stuff of his parables?

The short answer is: not from some 'never never land', but
from the real world all around him.

It has been observed that a study of the sayings-source we
call 'Q' would prove that our Lord was country-bred, so
redolent is it of all the sights and sounds of the natural world.
No less the parables reveal how many images, analogies, illustrations he took from the open book of Nature. 'The simplest
sights we met', writes Sir Edwin Arnold, after visiting Palestine:

> The simplest sights we met
> The sower flinging seed on loam and rock;
> The darnel in the wheat; the mustard tree
> That hath its seed so little, and its boughs
> Wide-spreading; and the wandering sheep; and nets
> Shot in the wimpled waters,—drawing forth

[1] T. W. Manson, *The Teaching of Jesus*, 73.

> Great fish and small,—these and a hundred such
> Seen by us daily, never seen aright,
> Were pictures for him from the book of life,
> Teaching by parable.

But the five parables mentioned here by no means exhaust the evidence. Think of the weather signs—the cloud in the west foretokening rain, the south wind with its promise of heat; or the budding figtree which is the harbinger of summer; or all the images of men going forth to till and reap the fields: the ploughman with his eyes fixed straight ahead; the seed growing secretly, first the blade, then the ear, then the full grain in the ear; and then the fields white with a plentiful harvest, with the labourers putting in the sickle because the time for reaping has come. All these things reveal the mind of One who knew the life of the countryside at first-hand, and loved it because it disclosed the presence and power of the Father who sent his rain on the just and the unjust and made his sun rise on the evil and on the good.

(Sometimes today city-bred ministers, preaching to rural congregations, use pastoral illustrations, only to exhibit their own ignorance and court the countryman's mockery. But the great Master of preaching makes no such blunders. Your European — or American — farmer today, reading that the Sower cast his seed on the unploughed stubble, might suppose that Jesus had erred. He would be wrong, for this is precisely what happens in Palestine, where sowing *precedes* ploughing.)[1]

Still larger, in the parables, bulks the human scene and the life of ordinary men, women and children in home or farm or market. It has often been remarked that The Leaven must go back to the time when Jesus watched 'Mary his mother' hiding the yeast in 'three measures of meal', or that The Playing Children takes us back to a Nazareth street where the lads and lasses played 'make believe' at weddings or at funerals. For proof that the Prodigal Son was no unreal or uncommon figure, we have only to read two contemporary papyrus letters about actual prodigals. 'Our son Castor', write the parents of

[1] Jeremias, *The Parables of Jesus* (revised edn. 1963), 11 f.

one sadly, 'has squandered all his own property by riotous living.' The other confesses: 'I know that I have sinned.'

The people of the parables are real people,[1] acting in character. Here are two men building houses; but one has the wit to choose a solid site, the other has not, with what consequences we know. Here are two more, with a dispute between them, and bent on taking the matter to the court. Here is 'a gay Sadducee', clad in purple and lawn and 'faring sumptuously every day'; and here a rich farmer, building still bigger granaries to house increasing crops, and dreaming of a carefree old age when, all of a sudden, he drops down dead. At the other end of the scale, we find the farmer's man who, having done a hard day's work in the field, must fall to and prepare his master's supper before he can 'get a bite' himself; or the labourers who hang about in the market-place because no man has hired them. More exciting characters are the peasant who, in ploughing a field, uncovers treasure-trove and promptly buys the field at its market value and makes his fortune; or the merchant who, one day, after long searching, lights on a truly superb pearl, and parts with all his other specimens to buy it.

But the realism of the parables goes even further than this, for many of them must have been founded on actual happenings. When Jesus used the similitude of The Burglar, no doubt the whole town was talking about a recent case of housebreaking. Behind the story of The Ten Virgins lay the story of an actual wedding at which some guests, forgetting to make proper preparations, turned up late and found the door shut in their faces. H. B. Tristram[2] has described a *kadi* (or judge) and a widow in Nisibis uncommonly like the two people in Christ's story. Probably the Galilee of AD 30 knew a rascally manager who was the original of The Unjust Steward; and the tale of The Wicked Vinedressers rings true of a Galilee

---

[1] And his animals real animals. 'His parables are not like Aesop's fables. His lost sheep has no arguments; his lily is not a Solomon, though it is better dressed.'

T. R. Glover, *The Conflict of Religions*, 123.

[2] *Eastern Customs in Bible Lands*, 228.

which we know was cursed at that time by absentee landlords and agrarian discontent. We may well hesitate to follow those who think that Jesus himself was the man 'who fell among thieves'; but brigandage of this kind was common enough then on the dangerous twenty miles that lay between Jerusalem and Jericho.

In all this one thing is clear. Jesus believed that human life with all its faults and frailties could furnish pointers and analogies of the Kingdom of God, and that our human care and concern could figure forth, however faintly, the care and concern of God. If this is so, must we not say that the image of God in man, though marred by sin, is still a reality? Barthians who call God 'the unheard of, mysterious Person who cannot be recognized anywhere in the world' do not seem to have the mind of Christ on this point. Concerned to assert that God's majestic reality cannot be enclosed within the obvious appearances of life, they tend to shroud in grim denial the bright encouragement offered by such parables as The Asking Son, The Friend at Midnight, and The Unjust Judge. 'If you then being evil, know how to give good gifts to your children, how much more . . .' It is helpful to learn that the great theologian of Basel, reacting from his earlier extremes, is now ready to talk about the 'humanity of God'.

5. Our last question is: Is the tradition of the parables trustworthy?

The answer is 'yes', for various reasons. For one thing, in many parables the Palestinian background and the Aramaic idiom still traceable in the Greek betoken the primitive and original. An excellent example of both these features is provided by the parable of The Sower. We have already seen that it implies the Palestinian farmer's practice of sowing his seed on the *un*ploughed stubble. As for its Aramaicized Greek, we need only quote Dr. Matthew Black:[1] 'Here in Mark we may speak with confidence of a literal translation Greek version of a parable of Jesus.' For a second point, the parables reveal everywhere Jesus' own highly individual way of thinking and

---

[1] *An Aramaic Approach*, 45.

speaking—the daring faith in God, the picturesque outlook on man and nature, the swift little surprises of thought so characteristic of him, the occasional flashes of irony and humour. All these are self-authenticating: the speech 'bewrays' the Man. And, for a third and general consideration, it is worth observing that great parables are evidently so difficult to create that it is hard to name another person in history with more than one or two good ones to his credit.

But if the general tradition is to be trusted, this does not mean that no changes overtook the parables in the forty or fifty years which elapsed before they were committed to writing.[1] Here we have learned much from the Form Critics with their emphasis on the part played in the transmission of the Gospel tradition by the believing, worshipping and witnessing community. We are to think (the Form Critics tell us) of the parables, in the period of the oral tradition, circulating singly or in pairs and taking a second lease of life as the early Church impressed them into her service. For what did the early Christians use them? For preaching and teaching, exactly as we use them today. The parables became vehicles of Christian nurture, exhortation and apologetic.

Thus the parables, in the earliest days, had two settings— their original setting in the ministry of Jesus, and their later one in the life of the early Church. How did the Church treat them? The Gospels supply the answer. Some they 're-audienced'. The Lost Sheep, on Jesus' lips a parable of the redemptive joy of God addressed to the Pharisees, became in Matt. 18 (the Church chapter) a summons to the disciples to pastoral concern for erring members. Others they 're-employed' for hortatory purposes. The parable of The Defendant, originally (as we shall see later) a parable of Crisis, has become in Matt. 5 a call to the Christian to 'make it up' with his estranged brother. Others they 're-applied' to their own eschatological situation 'between the times' (the Resurrection and the *Parousia*). Thus The Ten Virgins, which had been in Christ's mouth a rousing 'Be prepared!' to Israel in view of

[1] Jeremias, *The Parables of Jesus*, Chapter 2.

the great crisis set in motion by his ministry, has become, in the Church's use, a call to be ready for Christ's Second Advent.

In two cases the Church (or the Evangelists) conflated originally separate parables. St Matthew has tacked on The Wedding Garment, originally an independent parable, to The Wedding Feast. In Luke's parable of The Pounds (which corresponds to Matthew's Talents) we can detect at three or four points the intrusion of another parable about a man who went abroad to claim a kingdom.

In three cases (The Tares, The Dragnet and The Sower) we find that in the process of transmission interpretations have been appended to these parables which sound very like early Christian expositions of them. Finally, in a number of instances we can see how the Church *generalized* the meaning of a parable by adding a saying of Jesus which did not originally belong to the parable.[1] The saying about 'the last being first, and the first, last' which stands at both the beginning and end of Matthew's Labourers in the Vineyard, is one such example. Another is the addition at the close of The Pharisee and the Publican of the words: 'For every one who exalts himself will be humbled, but he who humbles himself will be exalted.'

Some people find these facts disconcerting to their faith. They are loth to admit that the early Christians could have so re-employed and re-applied the Lord's parables for their own purposes. But shall we fault the first Christians for turning the parables into vehicles of Christian nurture and edification when we do not dissimilar things today in Christian pulpits every Sunday? No, the recognition of these things should not shake our general confidence in the tradition of the parables. It simply means that when we try to restore some of the parables to their original 'life setting' in the ministry of Jesus, we must make allowance for the Church's usage. On the general question of trustworthiness the verdicts of two great scholars may be accepted:

'That a few of the parables have undergone modification in

[1] See Appendix 4.

the process of transmission', writes Denney,[1] 'is undeniable: but there is no part of the Gospel tradition in which we can be surer of our contact with the mind of Jesus than the tradition of the parables.'

'The student of the parables,' says Jeremias,[2] 'as they have been transmitted to us in the first three Gospels, may be confident that he stands upon a particularly firm historical foundation. The parables are a fragment of the original rock of the tradition.'

[1] *The Expositor*, August 1911, 136.   [2] Op. cit., 11.

2

THE STORY OF INTERPRETATION

FROM THE apostolic age to the present day Christian scholars have been engaged in interpreting the parables. All down these nineteen centuries one question has dominated the discussion: how much of the parable is really significant? That is: does a parable exist to make one point or many? To allegorize, or not to allegorize, that has been the question.

In the story of interpretation we are now going to sketch, the most diverse answers have been given to the question. The greatest Biblical scholar of antiquity, Origen of Alexandria, allegorizes the parables inveterately and, we might almost say, illimitably, firmly persuaded that this is the treatment they require. On the other hand, the most scientific student of the parables in the nineteenth century, Jülicher of Marburg, comes down on allegorizing like a hammer, insisting that a true parable contains one point and one point only—only to find himself in turn criticized for too much 'vigour and rigour'.

Moreover, all down the centuries the interpretation of the parables by the Church's scholars has been coloured, and often vitiated, not only by their doctrine of the Holy Scripture but also by their theology. And in this, as St Paul would say, 'all have sinned', Protestants as well as Catholics. Take the doctrine of Scripture first. If you believe, as the Fathers and the medieval scholars did, in the plenary inspiration of the Scriptures, and that the Old and New Testaments tell one story, in a complete and uncritical kind of unity, you will find no difficulty in saying that the wounded traveller in The Good Samaritan is Adam and that Christ himself is The Good Samaritan. Or consider how a man's theology may influence his exegesis of the parables. 'Grand old Martin Luther' is a

21

wonderful expositor of the Scriptures; but when he comes to explain the parables, you will observe how his favourite doctrine of 'justification by faith' keeps 'breaking into them', like 'cheerfulness' in the story of the man who told Dr Johnson that he too 'had tried to be a philosopher'. Even modern exegetes like Jülicher who reckon themselves truly scientific, cannot keep their own Liberal views of Christ out of their understanding of the parables. And doubtless the 'neo-orthodox' of the twentieth century succumb to the same temptation!

In the later chapters of this book we hope to show what a flood of new light modern scholarship has thrown on the parables; but, if we are to get the whole subject in proper perspective and avoid past errors, we must start with a back glance at the long history of interpretation. What, for instance, did Church Fathers like Irenaeus and Tertullian, Origen and Augustine, make of the parables? Did the Church's view of them alter materially in the middle ages? How did the new insights of the Reformation affect the Reformers' understanding of the parables? How did the seventeenth-century Protestant scholastics handle them? By the beginning of the nineteenth century the new Biblical criticism had begun to throw down its challenge in strong earnest. What did the Liberal theologians make of them? And so into this chaotic and calamitous twentieth century with all its theological changes: the eclipse of liberalism, the rise of neo-orthodoxy, existentialism, form criticism, realized eschatology, demythologizing, etc., etc.

We will divide the story into three parts:

1. From the apostolic age to the end of the middle ages;
2. The Reformation and after;
3. The modern period.

I

We may start by saying that from New Testament times to the Reformation, allegory in one form or another supplied the chief key for the interpretation of the parables. Basically, allegory means the interpretation of a text in terms of something else, regardless of what that something else may be. The method was Greek, and older than Plato. Homer, whose works became a kind of Bible for the Greek races, was the first author to receive allegorical treatment. If the literal sense of Homer yielded an unworthy meaning—and the amours of the Olympian deities were calculated to shock the spiritually sensitive—it became the fashion to dig deep and find a convenient 'under meaning' (*hyponoia*). Later, in this way, the Stoics succeeded in finding the 'elements' of the universe hidden in Homer: Zeus signifying the upper air; Hera, the lower air; Poseidon, representing water; and Athena, the earth. But for our immediate purpose the important name among the allegorizers is that of Philo of Alexandria, whose allegorizing ingenuity in the first century AD enabled him to reconcile the faith of Israel with Greek philosophy. With Philo, who has been called 'the most prominent modernist of ancient Judaism', Greek allegorizing found a firm foothold in the Jewish exegetical tradition, with what consequences for the interpretation of the parables we shall see later.

In the New Testament itself allegory is not commonly employed—except in Hebrews which may have had Alexandrian affiliations. Yet the first attempts to apply it to the parables may be seen in the interpretations added to The Sower, The Tares and The Dragnet. (Later, Origen was to justify his allegorizing by appeal to the example set by the evangelists.) You may also detect the beginnings of allegorical interpretation in Matthew—especially in his understanding of The Marriage Feast (Matt. 22) where probably 'the king' represents God, and 'the king's son', Christ, or in The Ten Virgins which doubtless he understood as an allegory of the return of Christ the heavenly bridegroom (Matt. 25). But, these things aside, the only real allegories in the New Testament are Paul's allegories of Sarah and Hagar (Gal. 4) and of The Olive Tree (Rom. 11)—and our Lord's tale about The Wicked Vinedressers (Mark 12); of which more anon.

In the second century allegory found increasing favour. A book like *The Shepherd of Hermas* (written 140-155), though it never mentions a parable of Jesus, shows how churchmen had begun to use allegory for their own purposes. But so also did the Gnostics who poured into the parables their own wild fancies and forced men like Irenaeus and Tertullian to rescue them from this abuse. Not that Irenaeus and Tertullian forswore the use of allegory—far from it—but they made the apostolic rule of faith their norm of interpretation.

Irenaeus (*c*.130-*c*.200) has left us several specimens of his work on the parables. In The Hid Treasure, for example, he takes the field to signify the Scriptures, while the treasure is Christ himself.[1] Much more elaborate is his exegesis of The Labourers in the Vineyard.[2] The first call to the workers represents the beginning of the created world, while the second symbolizes the Old Covenant. The third call represents Christ's Ministry. The long lapse of time in which we now live is the fourth call, while the final call symbolizes the end of time. The vineyard is righteousness; the householder, the Spirit of God; and the *denarius,* or 'penny', is immortality.

If we judge Irenaeus no tiro in the art of allegorizing, Tertullian (160-220) can show him a thing or two. His exposition of The Prodigal Son[3] reveals him at his best—or worst. The Elder Son in the story is the Jew; the Younger, the Christian. The patrimony of which the Younger claimed his share is that knowledge of God which a man has by his birthright. The citizen in the far country to whom he hired himself is the devil. The robe bestowed on the returning prodigal is that sonship which Adam lost at the Fall; the ring is the sign and seal of baptism; the feast is the Lord's Supper. And who is 'the fatted calf', slain for the feast, but the Saviour himself?

It was not in Gaul or North Africa, however, but in Alexandria—Philo's city—that the allegorization of the parables was to be developed into a fine art. Here the two important names are those of Clement (150-215) and Origen (185-254), his suc-

---

[1] *Against Heresies,* Book IV, Chap. xxvi. I.
[2] Op. cit., IV, xxxvi. 7.   [3] *On Modesty*, Chap. 9.

cessor as head of the great catechetical school. To understand
their methods of exegesis, we must remember not only that
both these scholars held to the verbal infallibility of the Scriptures but also that allegory was the accepted exegetical device
of the time. In Clement, it has been said, 'we find the allegorical method of Philo baptized into Christ'.[1] One example of his
exegesis must suffice. In The Mustard Seed he sees a repre-
sentation of Christ. 'The productiveness of the seed's nature',
he declares,[2] signifies Christ's manifold influence. And then,
mixing *materia medica* with moralizing, he observes: 'mustard
lessens bile, that is, anger, and stops inflammation, that is,
pride. From this Word (*i.e.* Christ the seed) springs the true
health of the soul and its eternal happy temperament.'

But if any man deserves the name of *maestro* in this art that
man is Origen. Scripture, he held, might bear no less than three
senses. As man is body, soul and spirit, so is Holy Writ. And
so any particular passage might have at once a literal meaning,
a moral one, and a spiritual one. Consider the mustard seed.
What is its literal sense? Obviously the physical grain of mustard. On the moral level, it means faith. And on the spiritual
level, it means the Kingdom of God. There is nothing specially
fantastic about this. It is when Origen comes to expound parables like The Labourers in the Vineyard or The Good Samaritan that his allegorical *expertise* almost takes our breath away.

This is how he explains the first of these parables.[3] The first
shift of workers signifies the generations from creation to
Noah; the second, those from Noah to Abraham; the third,
those from Abraham to Moses; the fourth, those from Moses
to Joshua; the fifth, those up to the time of Christ. The householder is God, while the penny represents salvation.

Hear him next on The Good Samaritan.[4]

The man who fell among thieves is Adam. As Jerusalem
represents heaven, so Jericho, to which the traveller journeyed,
is the world. The robbers are man's enemies, the devil and his
minions. The priest stands for the Law, the Levite for the pro-

[1] R. M. Grant, *The Bible in the Church*, 65.   [2] *Paid.*, 1.11.
[3] Bugge, *Die Hauptparabeln Jesu*, 283.   [4] Bugge, op. cit., 400 *f*.

phets. The good Samaritan is Christ himself. The beast on which the wounded man was set, is Christ's body which bears the fallen Adam. The inn is the Church; the two pence, the Father and the Son; and the Samaritan's promise to come again, Christ's Second Advent.

What shall we say of this sort of exegesis? *C'est pittoresque, mais ce n'est pas l'histoire*! Yet Origen, the greatest Biblical scholar of antiquity, was persuaded that this was the only right way to do it. 'What we have to do', he said,[1] 'is to transform the sensible Gospel into a spiritual one. For what would the sensible Gospel amount to if it were not developed into a spiritual one? It would be of little account or none . . . Our whole energy is to be directed to the effort to penetrate to the deep things of the meaning of the Gospel.'

We might imagine that in Origen's treatment of The Good Samaritan ingenuity could go no further; yet a hundred and fifty years later we find the great Augustine (354-430) himself out-origening Origen! For now we learn[2] that the wounded traveller is fallen man, half alive in his knowledge of God and half dead in his slavery to sin; the binding up of his wounds signifies Christ's restraint of sin; the pouring in of oil and wine, the comfort of good hope and the exhortation to spirited work. The innkeeper, dropping his *incognito*, is revealed as the Apostle Paul; and the two pence turn out to be the two commandments of love.

If this is not enough, we may quote his exposition of The Barren Fig Tree. The fig tree, he tells us, is the human race, for when man first sinned, he covered his limbs with fig leaves! The three years signify the time before the giving of the Law, the time under the Law, and the time of Gospel grace. The gardener is any saint who prays God to spare all sinners. The digging about and dunging of the tree mean the teaching of repentance and lowliness. If we ask why, he answers that, when we repent, we do so in filthy robes, and, after all, is not dung filthy as well as fruitful?[3]

[1] *Comm. Joh.*, 1.10.   [2] *Quaestiones Evangeliorum*, 2.19.
[3] *Sermons*, LX.

With engaging frankness Augustine tells us that he enjoyed the exercise of ingenuity which this method of exegesis affords, and adds that, as a preacher, he found that it gripped his hearers' attention. How many preachers since might have made like Augustinian confessions!

Fantastic? Yes! But before we moderns, with our up-to-date exegetical tools, grow too superior, we do well to remember two things. First, as we said already, allegorizing was the accepted exegesis of the day in Alexandria—if you like, the contemporary Higher Criticism. Second, this insistence of Origen and his friends that every passage of Scripture had a 'spiritual' meaning enabled them to accept passages in the Bible which otherwise might have seemed 'unworthy' of God.

Nevertheless, when all is said in extenuation of the Alexandrian exegetes, it remains that they carried the art of allegorizing to the point of absurdity. And if it be asked, 'Did none of the early Fathers realize that this was no proper way to treat the parables?', the answer is: the men of Antioch did.

To a man the Antiochene Fathers set their faces against allegorizing, resolved to discover what the sacred author meant and to be sure that all spiritual applications wrung from the text accorded with his intention. Theodore of Mopsuestia (350-428), one famous pupil of the Antioch school, wrote no less than five volumes against the allegorizers. But the greatest Antiochene name is that of John Chrysostom, the 'golden-mouthed' (347-407).

'Interpret the elements in the parables that are urgent and essential . . . do not waste time on all the details . . . seek out the scope for which the parable was designed . . . and be not overbusy with the rest.' So Chrysostom counselled,[1] and in his *Homilies* he practised what he preached. Discoursing on The Marriage Feast,[2] he says there is no need to seek out special meanings for 'the dinner, the oxen and the fat calves', since these but provide the necessary background to the tale. And he has a refreshing way of going for the main point of each parable. Thus (he says) The Mustard Seed and The

[1] *Matt. Hom.* lxiv, 3.　　　　　　　　[2] Ibid., lxix, 1.

Leaven deal with the divine power of the Gospel,[1] as The Hid Treasure and The Costly Pearl suggest its great value. The wise builder similarly represents the virtuous man, as the foolish stands for the immoral.[2] And so on. It is not claimed that in his exegesis Chrysostom always scored a bull's eye; but, generally speaking, he has his sights trained on the heart of the parable. Says a recent writer:[3] 'He comments sensibly, rarely seeking for allegorical meanings, with a superb sense of authority, in a rich prose that flashes like the prose of John Donne.' Not without reason Aquinas said that he would rather possess Chrysostom's *Homilies* than be master of Paris.

It was the misfortune of history that Alexandrian allegory was destined to prevail over the good sense of Antioch. The ecclesiastical courts discredited Theodore's writings, and Chrysostom was condemned as a heretic. But, church politics apart, the Latin student (as Miss Beryl Smalley has said)[4] found that the Alexandrian exegesis answered to his emotional need, whereas the Antiochene seemed to him unemotional and cold.

How did the parables fare in what we call the middle ages? The period now to be briefly covered is that which begins with Gregory the Great (540-604), the last of the Latin Doctors of the Church and the first medieval Pope, and ends with Nicholas of Lyra (1270-1340) who influenced Luther—

> *Si Lyra non lyrasset*
> *Lutherus non saltasset.*

In all, the period covers nearly a thousand years.

Throughout this time dogmatic theology rather than scriptural exegesis was the main interest, and in matters of interpretation the medieval scholars and preachers relied for the most part on the work of the Fathers like Origen and Augustine. 'The soberest scholarship of the middle ages', says Miss Smalley, 'derived its permit and its direction ultimately from Alexandria'.[5] This meant the continuation—and even exten-

---

[1] *Matt. Hom.* xlvii, 2. [2] Ibid., xxiv, 4.
[3] Robert Payne, *The Holy Fire*, 237.
[4] *The Study of the Bible in the Middle Ages*, 19. [5] Op. cit., 12.

sion—of the allegorical method. Indeed, the medieval exegetes went one better than Origen. Origen's 'spiritual' sense of Scripture they divided into the 'allegorical' and the 'anagogical'. This, with the 'literal' and the 'moral' gave a grand total of four senses!

From time to time men arose to protest against this wholesale discovery of 'spiritual' meanings in the Scripture; but, for the most part, where the parables were concerned, it was a case of 'the mixture as before'. Thus in the eighth century 'the greatest scholar in Christendom',[1] the Venerable Bede of Jarrow (673-735), when he discusses the parables, leans upon Ambrose and Augustine, Irenaeus and Origen. 'The Prodigal', he says,[2] 'is worldly philosophy which, unsatisfied, having deserted its true master Christ, yet hungers after truth, while faithful Christians receive the bread of the Word in the Father's house'. As for The Labourers in the Vineyard,[3] the householder is God; the vineyard is the Church; the hired men, the saints of all ages; and the penny, the divinity of Christ.

At the other end of the middle ages stands St Thomas Aquinas (1225-74), author of the *Catena Aurea*, a 'golden chain' of quotations from twenty-two Greek and twenty Latin writers, which served as a commentary on the Gospels. These specimens from the garden of the Fathers are meant, among other things, to provide guidance on the interpretation of the parables. Aquinas's treatment of The Two Builders will furnish a good example of his exegesis.[4] The wise builder is Christ who founded his house, the Church, upon the rock of faith. The foolish builder is the devil whose house—all unbelievers—he built upon the sands of unbelief. The rain is either the Holy Spirit or the spirit of the devil, according to the house on which it fell. Likewise, the winds are either the angels or unclean spirits; and the floods signify either Christian teachers or professors of worldly wisdom.

But perhaps the best illustration of the Church's practice in

---

[1] Winston S. Churchill, *History of the English-speaking Peoples*, I, 12.   [2] J. T. McNeill, *The Interpreter's Bible*, I, 117.
[3] Bugge, op. cit., 284.   [4] *Catena* I, part I, 291 f.

the middle ages is provided by an actual sermon preached by a friar in an English country church about 1150. Using the friar's 'notes', Conrad Pepler[1] pictures the scene.

'It is now the twelfth Sunday after Pentecost. The bright August sun picks out the East window which is edged with small scenes from the parables, and among them we can see the Lord as the Good Samaritan. The New Testament lesson for the day is from this same parable, and the friar announces his text with care . . .

'Then he goes on to show that it was man who went down from Jericho when Adam sinned and fell among demons:

' "The priest passed down the same way, when the order of patriarchs followed the path of mortality. The priest left him wounded, having no power to aid the human race while himself wounded with sins. The Levite went that way, in as much as the order of prophets also had to tread the path of death . . . The Lord was The Good Samaritan. He went down this way when he came from heaven into this world."

'And the preacher allegorizes the parable down to the smallest detail. "Two pence are given to the innkeeper when the doctors are raised on high by scriptural knowledge and temporal honour." '

Could anything better show how current theology might influence the interpretation of the parables? The medieval scholars liked to quote Augustine's dictum: 'The Scripture teaches nothing but the Catholic Faith.' This is precisely what our friar makes the parable do. Moreover, if we study his exposition, we can trace an allegorizing line that goes back at least to Origen.

To sum up. If sound exegesis means beginning from the plain meaning of the parable in its original 'life-setting' in the ministry of Jesus in the endeavour to discover and apply some deep truth about the Kingdom of God, the bulk of the exegesis we have surveyed, however edifying to the faithful, must be called unsound. It is told of the Emperor Galerius that he once watched an archer firing twenty successive arrows at a target

---

[1] *The Interpretation of the Bible* (Ed. Dugmore), 26-28.

and missing with the lot. 'May I congratulate you', said Galerius to the luckless archer afterwards, 'on your splendid talent for missing?' Would it be unfair to say of the exegetes we have been studying—with of course shining exceptions like Chrysostom—that, where the true meaning of the parables was at stake, they showed a like remarkable flair for missing?

II

Then came the Renascence and the Reformation. What happened is familiar and needs no long recital: the revival of classical learning; the invention of printing; the revolt against Rome; the new interest in the original languages of the Bible; the appearance of vernacular translations like Luther's, etc., etc. All this meant that Scripture became the supreme authority and that its interpretation was more and more liberated from church tradition. With the new scholarly tools supplied by Renascence 'humanists' like Erasmus, Biblical exegesis took a new lease of life; and in theory, at any rate, everyman now became, with the Holy Spirit's help, his own interpreter of Holy Writ. (This was not an unmixed blessing; for now it became increasingly possible for this same everyman to make himself a public nuisance with his private opinions!)

Thus the way was prepared for a new approach by the Reformation scholars to the interpretation of the parables. Grammars and lexicons now became indispensable aids for exegetes; a fresh emphasis was laid on the plain and obvious meaning of Scripture; and since Reformers like Luther and Calvin knew the difference between the words of the Bible and the Word of God, they did not feel compelled to find in the details of the parables subtle 'under meanings' which were never in the mind of Jesus when he uttered them.

What did Luther and Calvin make of the parables?

We all know that Martin Luther (1483-1546) was a mighty expositor of the Scriptures who brought to his task all the insights of experiential religion, especially of the Pauline kind. But it must be confessed that, for all his freshness and power, his principles were sometimes better than his practice, at least where the interpretation of the parables was concerned. When we find him repudiating the medieval fourfold sense of Scripture, dismissing the allegorizers as 'clerical jugglers performing monkey tricks' (*Affenspiel*), saying hard things about Origen's exegesis ('worth less than dirt'), and expressing a strong preference for the literal (or 'grammatical') sense, we are filled with great expectations. In practice, however, Luther remained quite hospitable to the allegories of the Fathers, and his exposition of The Good Samaritan shows as many 'monkey tricks' as Origen's.[1]

His other sin as an exegete was his *penchant* for finding his favourite evangelical principle of *sola fide* in passages where it would not readily occur to most of us. A good example of this—as well as of his ability to make the parables speak to his contemporaries—is to be found in his treatment of The Great Supper.[2]

'The sum of the parable', he says, 'is that the Gospel is preached and published throughout the whole world, but few receive and embrace it. Supper here means the rich and sumptuous feast which God made through Christ in the Gospel. The servants are the apostles sent to proclaim it. The phrase "all things are now ready" means that the Father has paid the price of all things. The reason why the contemptuous guests refused the invitation was that they had not enough faith to stake all on the Gospel, leaving work and wife and all earthly concerns. The first to be invited were the Jews; then came the Gentiles' turn. And the guests who, when bidden to the feast, did not come, signify those who think they will obtain the Supper by their own good works.'

We may be able to pick exegetical holes in this today; but what a vast improvement it is on some of the allegorical arabesques we have been studying! For, with all his faults as

[1] *Sermons by Martin Luther* (Tr. by James Kerr), 207-223.
[2] Op. cit., 136-141.

an interpreter, Luther has a sense of what is vital in New Testament religion, and an eye for the main point of a parable. No better example could be found than his comment on The Unjust Steward.[1] Let us not (he says) fall into the error of imagining that everything in the story is significant. If we did, we would be encouraged to go about 'cheating our masters', as the steward did. No, the point to fasten on is 'the cleverness of the steward who saw his own advantage and so well and wisely achieved it'. And this, beyond any doubt, is the point on which the original Teller of the story meant his hearers to focus their attention.

The other great Reformer, John Calvin (1509-64), was the best interpreter of the parables since Chrysostom. Admirably equipped for his task by his knowledge both of the classical tongues and of the Fathers, he brings to his exposition a rare percipience and lucidity. The allegorizings of the Fathers he pronounces 'idle fooleries'. Since it is the first business of a commentator to let his author say what he does say, 'we ought to have a deeper reverence for Scripture than to reckon ourselves at liberty to disguise its natural meaning'.[2] And in his own commentaries he generally goes, arrow-straight, for this 'natural meaning' of a parable, setting down the central point in one short, clear sentence.

As, for example, à propos of The Unjust Steward:[3]

'How stupid it is to want to interpret it in every detail! Christ simply meant that the children of this world are more diligent in their concern for their own fleeting interests than the sons of light for their eternal well-being.'

Or of The Tares:[4]

'In my opinion, the design of the parable is simply this: so long as the pilgrimage of the Church in the world continues, bad men and hypocrites will mingle in it with the good and upright, that the children of God may be armed with patience,

---

[1] E. Mülhaupt, Luther's *Evangelien-Auslegung*, II, 677.
[2] *Harmony on Matthew, Mark and Luke*, III, 63.
[3] Ibid., II, 177.   [4] Ibid., II, 119.

2

and in the midst of offences fitted to disturb them may preserve steadfast faith.'

Or this on The Farmer and his Man (Luke 17.7-10):[1]

'The object of this parable is to show that all the zeal manifested by us in discharging our duty does not put God under any obligation to us by any sort of merit; for, as we are his property, so he on his part can owe us nothing.'

It is idle to fault Calvin because he has not the modern scholar's interest in the original setting of each parable, or because he does not examine critically the differences between two versions of a parable (e.g. The Great Supper, found in both Matthew and Luke). Source criticism and form criticism, which shed light on such questions, were things of which neither he nor any of his contemporaries knew anything. Calvin is chiefly concerned to make each parable speak to the needs of his people; but his quick insight, good sense and admirable clarity entitle him to a place among the greatest expositors of the parables.

Before we leave the Reformation times, we ought to mention a Roman Catholic scholar who did excellent work on the parables. Juan Maldonado, or Maldonatus (1533-83), was a Spanish Jesuit who taught in Paris. His commentaries on the Gospels reveal a deep distrust of allegorizing and a sense of what matters in a parable. The details, he insists, are often merely decorative and need no special interpretation. For an instance, he says that we must not try, when we study The Good Samaritan, to find hidden meanings in Jerusalem and Jericho. So far as Jesus was concerned, the man might have been travelling from 'Rome to Naples'. Many points in this story, he says of The Tares, have no special significance but are simply there because they are needed for the telling of the story. Then he adds, slily: 'Older commentators often identify the sleeping men in it with the bishops.' Elsewhere, after expounding The Importunate Widow, he says: 'This is the simple meaning. If you want an allegorical one, read Augustine

[1] Ibid., II, 194.

or Theophylact.' No wonder the Sorbonne accused him of heresy!

We have been discussing the new insights of the Reformation. Alas, they did not last long. The successors of the Reformers showed little of the freshness and acumen of Calvin and Luther, and in the seventeenth century a new era of scholasticism settled, like a depression, on the Protestant Church. The root of the trouble was that these 'neo-scholastics' came to identify the inspiration of the Bible with verbal inerrancy and to regard it as infallible even down to the vowel points of the Hebrew Bible. During this time there arose on the Continent the so-called 'historico-prophetical' school of Biblical interpreters. Best known among them were Johannes Cocceius (1603-69), a German theologian, and the Dutchman Campegius Vitringa (1659-1722). One basic belief of theirs was that many Scripture passages contained actual prophecies of the development of the Kingdom of God up to their own day. It was a corollary of this which led them to find in the parables of Jesus a part of the Kingdom's progressive development till the end of the world. Even the good and great Bengel (1687-1752), author of the famous *Gnomon* and pioneer in textual criticism, fell a victim to these 'futurist' speculations. When Vitringa tells us[1] that the pearl of great price is the Church of Geneva, we hardly need to be told that he is a Calvinist, though we may also surmise that John Calvin would have disowned his exegesis. But we need not spend further time on these neo-scholastics, since nobody nowadays—except perhaps some fundamentalists—reads the Bible or the parables in this historico-prophetical way.

III

The Modern Period

We pass to the modern period.

In the seventeenth and eighteenth centuries the Bible had

[1] See Trench, *Notes on the Parables*, 42.

been largely a holy book to be kept in a glass case. But in the beginning of the nineteenth century, with the rise of modern Biblical criticism, it was taken out of its glass case to be studied like any other book in the light of the latest knowledge. How did this affect the study of the Gospels?

It meant of course a mortal blow to the doctrine of verbal inspiration; but it meant also a fresh, unfettered approach to all the problems connected with the life of Jesus, including the parables. (The most brilliant account of all this is Albert Schweitzer's *Quest of the Historical Jesus.*)

The nineteenth century produced much writing about the parables. We have space to mention only three of the most important books.

A hundred years ago the standard English work on the parables was Archbishop Trench's *Notes on the Parables* (1841), a book still to be found on many ministers' library shelves. A marvellous mine of learning it was too; but when we open it today, we cannot help feeling that Trench is still in the middle ages and has learned nothing from Calvin. Fearful of the new Criticism, he keeps harking back to the Fathers for his views,[1] so that the Inn (in The Good Samaritan) is still the Church, the Robe (in The Prodigal Son) is imputed righteousness, and the Oil (in The Ten Virgins) is either faith or good works. He rightly says that the details in a parable are ancillary to the making of the main point; but in practice he tries to squeeze some spiritual meaning out of most of them. Thus in his study of The Seed Growing Spontaneously[2] he says that the main point is 'the secret invisible energy of the Divine Word' which unfolds itself irresistibly according to the laws of its being. But then he feels constrained to raise the question, who sowed the seed? It must be Christ, he guesses, only to encounter the phrase 'he knows not how'. Such ignorance cannot be predicated of Christ. Does then the man who sowed the seed signify Christ's ministers? Hardly, for they do not reap the harvest; Christ does. So, after all, the sower must be Christ,

[1] He practically repeats Augustine's interpretation of The Ten Virgins, 235-256.   [2] Op. cit., 278-281.

'though not exclusively', since 'he knows not how' applies to Christ's ministers. In short, the good archbishop is hard put to it to catch a hare which he should never have started running!

The first major book in English to harvest the fruits of the new criticism was A. B. Bruce's *Parabolic Teaching of Christ* (1882). Employing the methods of source criticism, he notes, for example, that Matthew's Marriage Feast and Luke's Great Supper may represent one parable differently reported by the first and third evangelists.[1] Allegorizing he boldly repudiates. The numbers in Luke's three parables of the Lost (Luke 15) are 'natural, not mysterious'. 'The hundred sheep are the property of a shepherd of average wealth; the ten pieces of money are the pecuniary possession of a woman in humble life; the two sons signify a family just large enough to supply illustrations of the two contrasted characters.'[2] Discussing The Lost Coin, he observes that it would be easy to say that the house is the Church; the woman, the Holy Spirit; the Coin, man stamped with the image of God but lying in the dust of sin; the candle, the Word of God. But (he comments) how much better to 'feel the human pathos of the parable as a story from real life, and then to make that pathos the connecting link between the natural and the spiritual world!'[3] This is typical. Bruce's faults are those of a man of his time—he is a Liberal, and so tends to think of the Kingdom of God as a Divine Commonwealth and to talk of 'the sweet reasonableness of Jesus',[4] in a way that reminds us of both Arnold and Renan. But he brings a true breath of Galilee back into the study of the parables. Of him his greatest pupil, James Denney, was to say, 'He let me see Jesus.'

The most famous book on the parables in this century came six years later from Germany: *Die Gleichnisreden Jesu* (Vol. I 1888, Vol. II 1899) by Adolf Jülicher. Jülicher sounded the death-knell of that allegorizing of the parables which had bedevilled their interpretation through the centuries.

[1] Op. cit., 460.
[2] Op. cit., 263.
[3] Op. cit., 279.
[4] Op. cit., 308, 328, 469.

First, said Jülicher, the parables of Jesus are similitudes, not allegories. Accordingly, each of them has one *tertium comparationis,* or point of likeness, not half a dozen.

Next, these similitudes Jesus employed to make his message plain and vivid to the multitudes. To this end he used apt and familiar comparisons from daily life. And therefore, if Mark 4.11f. says that Jesus employed parables to blind and befog his hearers, this is the early Church speaking, not Jesus.

Finally, in studying a parable, concentrate on the one central point of likeness, and consider the rest as dramatic machinery necessary for the telling of the tale. What about allegorizing the details? What about killing a man!

So thoroughly did Jülicher do his work that for a time it almost seemed as if he had spoken the last word on the parables. Then gradually scholars, of whom the two chief were C. A. Bugge[1] and Paul Fiebig,[2] began to see that, for all his great abilities, Jülicher had performed his task with too much Teutonic 'vigour and rigour'. His book had indeed two capital faults.

To begin with, Jülicher took his idea of a parable from Aristotle when he should have sought its prototype in the rabbinical *mashal.* Now the rabbis' parables are not all pure similitudes; some have allegorical elements; a few are allegories. Jülicher therefore erred in saying that Jesus' parables could not have contained allegorical elements.

Secondly, Jülicher said that a parable existed to make one point. But what kind of point? His answer was: a general moral truth—the more general the better. The point of The Sons of the Bridechamber was: 'Religious sentiment is valuable only if it expresses the proper sentiment' (II, 188). Of The Talents: 'A reward is only earned by performance' (II, 495). Of The Unjust Steward: 'Wise use of the present is the condition of a happy future' II, 511). Yet the Man who went about Galilee drawing these innocuous morals was eventually spiked to a Cross. There is something far wrong here. Would men have crucified a Galilean Tusitala who told picturesque stories to enforce prudential platitudes? Of course they would not! For all his merits Jülicher had left the task of interpretation half done.

Nevertheless, he had cleared the path for the next and revolutionary advance which came thirty-six years later with C. H. Dodd's *Parables of the Kingdom* (1935). This book made exegetical history; and we should agree with Joachim Jeremias who, a dozen years later, in his *Parables of Jesus* (1947)[1] was to dot the i's and stroke the t's of Dodd's exposition, that it is unthinkable there should ever be any retreat from Dodd's basic insights.

What, then, did Dodd and Jeremias do which Jülicher had not done? *They put the parables of Jesus back into their true setting, which is the ministry of Jesus seen as the great eschatological act of God in which he visited and redeemed his people.*

What a revolution in our understanding of the Gospels this sentence summarizes! We must pause to explain it, observing that the key word here is 'eschatological'.

In the thirty odd years that followed Jülicher's *magnum opus* New Testament science, following the lead of Johannes Weiss and Albert Schweitzer, made one very important advance. It discovered the true meaning of the Kingdom of God, which is the central concept of the Gospels and the theme of all the parables.

The Kingdom (*Basileia*: Aram. *malkutha*), which means the Rule or Reign of God, is an eschatological entity. Eschatology means the doctrine of the End (*eschaton*)—the End conceived as God's age-long and final purpose destined to be realized in the future and to give meaning to the whole travail of history. Now in Jewish thought the Reign of God is *the* great hope of the future. It is another name for the Good Time Coming, the Messianic Age; and it is essentially 'God's seed and not man's deed'. Thus, in reading the Gospels, we are to think of the

[1] Revised English edition published in 1963.

Kingdom not as some moral disposition in the heart of man or as some utopian society to be built by his efforts,[1] but as the decisive intervention of the living God on the stage of human history for man's salvation. This is the first point. The second is this. The heart of Jesus' message was that this royal intervention of God in human affairs was no longer a shining hope on the far horizon of history—but a *fait accompli*. The appointed time had fully come, said Jesus, the Kingdom had arrived, was invading history. The living God was laying bare his arm for men's salvation, was visiting his people decisively in grace and judgment. The Good News of the Gospel was therefore not so much a programme for human action as the proclamation of an act of God in Jesus Christ. This is what we know nowadays as 'realized eschatology'; and though the word 'realized' may not be the best one, the phrase makes sense of the Gospels and represents essential truth. Of course, there is terrific paradox here—the paradox of the relation between the Kingdom of God and the ministry of Jesus. Yet on our understanding of it depends our understanding not only of the Gospels but of the whole New Testament. What is the resolution of the paradox? It is that the meaning of 'realized eschatology' and the meaning of the Messianic ministry of Jesus are one and the same. Quite simply, the career of Jesus as the Servant Messiah, from Jordan to Calvary, *is* the Kingdom of God, God acting in his royal power, God visiting and redeeming his people.[2]

To this discovery was added in the 'twenties' of this century the work of the Form Critics. These scholars, of whom Dibelius and Bultmann were the most notable, taught us that in the period of the oral tradition the parables circulated singly or in pairs and were used by the early Christian preachers for preaching and teaching. Inevitably during this time the original setting of many of the parables was forgotten, as the

---

[1] The view of the Liberals, who offered us 'a kingdom of man with God to serve in it rather than a Kingdom of God with man to serve in it' (P. T. Forsyth, *The Cruciality of the Cross*, 31).
[2] See my *Introducing New Testament Theology*, Chapter 1.

church leaders re-applied them to their own situation and needs. The problem then before our scholars was to restore, if they could, these glorious pictures to their lost frames. This is the task which Dodd and Jeremias have accomplished for our generation.[1] They would be the last to claim that in all cases they have restored the parables to their original settings in the ministry of Jesus. But there can be no question that theirs is the right approach, and that they have enabled us to understand the parables as they have not been understood since apostolic times. Once recognize that the present settings of the parables in the Gospels are often those given them by the early Church, and that their original setting was one of 'realized eschatology', and you begin to see the parables, along with the miracles, as part and parcel of Jesus' great proclamation (or *kerygma*) that the Kingdom of God was invading history in his person and mission. It will be our task in the succeeding chapters so to arrange and elucidate the parables that the Kingdom themes which Jesus meant them to enforce will ring out clearly; and, if we will but use a little historical imagination, we may re-live the supreme crisis in which God visited Israel in blessing and in judgment through the ministry of Jesus, and the new Israel, which is the Church of Christ, was born.

[1] A notable precursor of Dodd and Jeremias was A. T. Cadoux in his *Parables of Jesus* (1930). Taught by the Form Critics, he sought the original 'life-setting' of each parable in the ministry of Jesus, and discovered that many were 'weapons of war' in his controversy with the Scribes and Pharisees.

3

THE COMING OF THE KINGDOM

OUR THEME in the following chapters will be the Gospel
in parable. We shall try to discover the original settings
of the parables in the ministry of Jesus and, by grouping
them together, hear again the authentic notes of the Galilean
Gospel. Jeremias proposes ten such groupings; but we shall
get along more simply with four, of which the first is 'The
Coming of the Kingdom'.

Jesus opened his Galilean Ministry by declaring that men
were standing on the threshold of a decisive hour of history:

The (appointed) time has fully come. The Reign of God has
arrived (*engiken*). Turn to God and believe in the good news
(Mark 1.15).[1]

The great prophecy of Isa. 52.7 was coming true:

> How beautiful upon the mountains
>   are the feet of the heralds,
> Who bring good news of peace,
>   news of salvation,
> Who say to Zion,
>   'Your God has become king.'

The era of the Kingdom of God whose advent prophets and
kings had yearned so long to see (Luke 10.23 f.; Matt. 13.16 f
Q), was beginning. There in their midst, for those who had
eyes to see, the Kingdom was already 'exercising its force'
(*biazetai*, Matt. 11.12). The summer of God's salvation was at
hand (Mark 13.28 f.);[2] his harvest was under way (Luke 10.2;
Matt. 9.37, Q).

[1] My translation.
[2] The similitude of The Budding Fig Tree probably reflects this time,
though the Church re-applied it to Christ's Second Coming. It says,
'Can't you see that the winter is over and the summer of salvation is
nigh?'

It is on this situation that our first group of parables forms a commentary.

A new era always throws up men who, fearful of the unknown future, would fain accommodate the new to the old. It must have been to men of this temper that Jesus replied in the twin parables of The Patch and The Wineskins:

No one sews a piece of unshrunk cloth on an old garment; if he does, the patch tears away from it, the new from the old, and a worse tear is made.

And no one puts new wine into old wineskins; if he does, the wine will burst the skins, and the wine is lost, and so are the skins (Mark 2.21 f.).

Such accommodation, says Jesus, is mere folly and waste of time. The old garment of Judaism will not stand such patching, nor can its outworn forms contain the fermenting wine of God's New Order. Every attempt to blend the grace of the Gospel with the legalism of the Law is foredoomed to failure. Here, in germ, is all the newness of the Gospel.

What then is the nature of this new and mysterious Kingdom? What are the laws of its growth? How does it work? And what is its God-appointed destiny? Such questions as these must have been asked; and in the so-called 'parables of growth' we have Jesus' answers.

Let us try to put ourselves back for a moment into the Galilee of Jesus' day. To the casual observer, the visible evidence for the new era seems to be only the poor, tiny, unremarkable band of Jesus' followers—not many wise, not many mighty. Can something so contemptibly small be pregnant with the great purpose of God? The parable of The Mustard Seed is Jesus' answer:

With what can we compare the kingdom of God, or what parable shall we use for it? It is like a grain of mustard seed which, when sown upon the ground, is the smallest of all the seeds on earth; yet when it is sown it grows up and becomes the greatest of all shrubs, and puts forth large branches, so that the birds of the air can make nests in its shade (Mark 4.30-32; cf. Luke 13.18 f., Q).

Have you ever noticed, asks Jesus, that every-day miracle in the natural world which transforms a tiny speck of mustard seed into a shrub ten feet tall where the wild birds come to nest? This miracle is about to be repeated in the spiritual world. The Reign of God may seem a fact of little importance; yet it is destined to span the earth with its empire and to embrace in its sweep the Gentiles from afar.[1]

But if 'small beginnings, great endings' is one law of the Kingdom's growth, there is another and its symbol is leaven:

> To what shall I compare the kingdom of God? It is like leaven which a woman took and hid in three measures of meal, till it was all leavened (Luke 13.20 f.; Matt. 13.33, Q).

The Kingdom, observe, is being compared not to leaven but to what happens when you put leaven into a batch of meal—a heaving, panting mass, swelling and bursting with bubbles, and all the commotion indicating something alive and at work below: in one phrase, a ferment, pervasive, dynamic, resistless. Even so when God's Rule enters the world, there must arise a disturbing process which ultimately nothing in the world can escape.

Let us pause here and get these two parables in proper perspective. A poem, popular not very long ago, had as its refrain:

> *Some call it evolution,*
> *And others call it God,*

and many people, regarding the Kingdom of God as a religious equivalent for the evolutionary process, construed our parables in terms of a social idealism. On such a reading, they seemed to predict the slow permeation of human society by the Rule of God. But this is to modernize Jesus and misapprehend him. The language here is not that of social idealism but of prophetic vision. And the true point of these parables, as Amos

---

[1] See Dan. 4.12; Ezek. 17.22 f.; 31.6. In such passages the great tree in whose branches the wild birds nest signifies a great empire embracing all peoples. Nor is this all. We know that the rabbis sometimes referred to the Gentiles as 'the birds of the air'.

Wilder has said,[1] is 'the amazing disproportion between the initial stages (of the Kingdom) and its outcome'. Jesus' concern is thus not with any human 'when' of the Kingdom's coming but with 'God's future' and man's destiny as a sharer in it. 'Unremarkable beginnings, unimaginable endings' might be a good summary. Our Lord is affirming that God's New Order is already in being, and by means of familiar images drawn from daily toil, is linking the lowly beginnings of his ministry with a final outcome which passes man's understanding.

Yet Jesus' hearers included men—one thinks of Simon the Zealot—who apparently were not satisfied even with this. With 'an irreligious solicitude for God', they wanted to accelerate the Kingdom's advance by direct action. These Jesus gently rebuked in the parable of The Seed Growing Spontaneously:

The kingdom of God is as if a man should scatter seed upon the ground, and should sleep and rise night and day, and the seed should sprout and grow, he knows not how. The earth produces of itself, first the blade, then the ear, then the full grain in the ear. But when the grain is ripe, at once he puts in the sickle, because the harvest has come (Mark 4.26-29).

It is a call to patience, with an assuring promise. 'God's Kingdom', Jesus says, 'is his care. Stage by stage, quietly but irresistibly, it grows to harvest, whether men will or no. Patience! Leave the issue to God.' Remark the splendid faith of Jesus. The seed has been sown; a new Divine energy has been released in the world; and Jesus can stand by and say, like Mark Antony in the play: 'Now let it work!'

But it is into a world of sinful men that God's Kingdom comes, as the parable of The Tares implies:

The kingdom of heaven may be compared to a man who sowed good seed in his field; but while men were sleeping, his enemy came and sowed weeds among the wheat, and went away. So when the plants came up and bore grain, then the weeds appeared also. And the servants of the householder came and said to him, 'Sir, did you not sow good seed in your field? How then has it weeds?' He said to them, 'An enemy has done this.' The servants said to him, 'Then do you want us to go and gather them?' But he

[1] *The Faith of the New Testament*, 95.

said, 'No, lest in gathering the weeds you root up the wheat along with them. Let both grow together until the harvest; and at harvest time I will tell the reapers, Gather the weeds first and bind them in bundles to be burned, but gather the wheat into my barn' (Matt. 13.24-30).

The parable sounds like Jesus' reply to a critic—probably a Pharisee (the very name meant 'separatist')—who had objected: 'If the Kingdom of God is really here, why has there not been a separating of sinners from saints in Israel?' 'Let both grow together until the harvest', is Jesus' reply. It is a warning against weeding. No farmer in his senses (the parable argues) tries to separate weeds from wheat while the crop is still growing. In plain prose: 'Leave the weeding of bad men from good to God at Judgment Day.' Or, as St Paul said, 'Judge not before the time' (I Cor. 4.5).

Clearly connected by content with The Tares is the parable of The Dragnet:

Again, the kingdom of heaven is like a net which was thrown into the sea and gathered fish of every kind; when it was full, men drew it ashore and sat down and sorted the good into vessels but threw away the bad (Matt. 13.47 f.).

This parable, however, probably answered the question not of some Pharisees but of those whom Jesus called to be 'fishers of men' (Mark 1.17)—his 'apprentices' in the work of the Kingdom.[1] To whom were they to go? Should they, in their missionary work, try to be selective? 'No more than a seine net', is the Lord's reply, 'You know how it sweeps all sorts of fish into its meshes, and it is only when the shore is reached, that sorting is done. So it is with the Kingdom of God. The time for separating will come, but inevitably, in its outreach, the Kingdom gathers in all sorts and conditions of men—lawbreakers and law-keepers, hot-blooded zealots and apocalyptic dreamers, reprobates and respectable folk.'

The Gospel tradition preserves yet another parable of growth, that of The Sower:

Listen! A sower went out to sow. And as he sowed, some seed fell along the path, and the birds came and devoured it. Other

[1] T. W. Manson, *The Teaching of Jesus*, 240.

seed fell on rocky ground, where it had not much soil, and immediately it sprang up, since it had no depth of soil; and when the
sun rose it was scorched, and since it had no root it withered
away. Other seed fell among thorns and the thorns grew up and
choked it, and it yielded no grain. And other seeds fell into good
soil and brought forth grain, growing up and increasing and yield-
ing thirtyfold and sixtyfold and a hundredfold (Mark 4.3-8).

What is the point of this most famous of the parables of
growth? Modern scholars, for the most part, lay the stress on
the abundant harvest, and not without reason: since tenfold
was reckoned a good harvest, yields of thirty-, sixty- and a
hundredfold signify a bumper harvest. (*Polus*, 'plentiful', is
Jesus' adjective in Matt. 9.37.) On this view, the parable carries
a ringing assurance for faint-hearted disciples. The parable
allows us to hear Jesus thinking aloud about the ups and downs
of the Galilean ministry. 'Despite all hazards and losses', he
says, 'the farmer reaps a splendid harvest. Even so, in spite of
all frustrations and failures, God's Rule advances, and his harvest exceeds all expectation. Courage! Have faith in God.'

Nevertheless much can also be said for the older exegesis
which found in the story a parabolic comment on 'Take heed
how you hear'. If we take it thus, Jesus is addressing the
multitudes. The seed which is the Good News of the Kingdom
(now a present reality) is all good, but for its fructifying everything depends on the soil into which it falls. So interpreted, it
is a parable on the responsibility of hearing the Gospel which
was meant to leave the hearer asking, 'What kind of soil am I?'

The images, so far, have mostly concerned seed-time and
harvest, clearly befitting a Galilean *milieu*. But pastoral images
of this kind, if taken by themselves, can easily give us a wrong
impression of Christ's ministry. Since Renan's day we have
tended to think of the Galilean ministry as a time of quiet
preaching and teaching in sharp contrast with his later career
when he was setting his face steadfastly to go to Jerusalem and
the Passion. We misunderstand the Galilean ministry if we
picture it only as a peaceful pastoral in which the serene wisdom of the Teacher accorded well with the birds and flowers
of Galilee. Such a picture we obtain only if we scale down the

miracles, evacuate the eschatological sayings of their mystery and depth, and regard the parables as picturesque stories about moral commonplaces. In fact, the ministry bore more resemblance to a campaign, a campaign against the powers of evil, in which there fights for us

> the Proper Man
> Whom God himself hath bidden,

a campaign which led Jesus eventually to his death-grapple with the powers of evil on the Cross and to the victory of the Resurrection.

The saying which best crystallizes this aspect of Christ's ministry is that wrung from him during the Beelzebub controversy: 'If I by the finger of God cast out demons, then the kingdom of God has come upon you' (Luke 11.20; Matt. 12.28, Q). It is against this background that the two little parables of The Divided Realm and The Strong Man Bound become intelligible:

How can Satan cast out Satan? If a kingdom is divided against itself, that kingdom cannot stand. And if a house is divided against itself, that house will not be able to stand. And if Satan has risen up against himself and is divided, he cannot stand, but is coming to an end.

But no one can enter a strong man's house and plunder his goods, unless he first binds the strong man; then indeed he may plunder his house (Mark 3.23-27; cf. Luke 11.21 f., Q).

Both these parables were born in the cut-and-thrust of that campaign in which Jesus not only proclaimed the presence of the Kingdom but in its name delivered men and women from demons and disease, so that he drew down on himself the charge of being in league with the powers of darkness. In the first parable he says in effect: 'Collusion with the arch-fiend, you say? But dog does not eat dog. The true interpretation of the facts is that the devil's realm, being divided, is doomed.' He makes a like point in The Strong Man Bound where his wording very significantly echoes Isa. 49.24 f. (a Servant passage).[1] It is the Servant Messiah who speaks: 'My exorcisms

[1] Compare Luke 11.22, 'He divides his spoils', with Isa. 53.12, 'He will divide the spoils with the strong'.

show that I am the devil's master. The captives of the mighty, as Isaiah foretold, are being taken and the prey of the tyrant rescued.'

To this phase of the ministry also belongs the parable of The Empty House:

When the unclean spirit has gone out of a man, he passes through waterless places seeking rest; and finding none, he says, 'I will return to my house from which I came.' And when he comes he finds it swept and put in order. Then he goes and brings seven other spirits more evil than himself, and they enter and dwell there; and the last state of that man becomes worse than the first (Luke 11.24-26; Matt. 12.43-45, Q).

The point of this grisly little story about demons is tolerably plain. Though a man is delivered from an evil spirit, he cannot be safe till God truly takes over the house of his life. Otherwise, the evil spirit will come back with renewed strength. Is Jesus warning an ex-demoniac of the danger of relapse, or telling a sinner that it is not enough merely to receive forgiveness, he must resolve to grow in holiness? Perhaps so; but is it not more likely that he is thinking of his people on whom 'the Kingdom of God had come' (Luke 11.20)? Their release from the powers of evil will be a blessing only if they are ready, by following him, to submit themselves to the beneficent power of God's Rule. Grace, like nature, abhors a vacuum; what is needed is, in Chalmers's phrase, 'the expulsive power of a new affection'.

The burden of the parables we have been considering is that the devil is being mastered and his realm tottering to its fall. And with this note of incipient victory we hear also in The Wedding Guests the concomitant note of joy:

Can the wedding guests fast while the bridegroom is with them? As long as they have the bridegroom with them, they cannot fast. The days will come, when the bridegroom is taken away from them, and then they will fast in that day (Mark 2.19 f.).

Pious men, noting the grave faces of the Baptist's disciples and of the Pharisees, thought that fasting would have better befitted Jesus and his men. 'Can the wedding guests (or "the groomsmen") fast while the bridegroom is with them?' Jesus replied, making a veiled claim to Messiahship. 'My disciples are as light-hearted as a wedding party. And why not? Kingdom time is no time for mourning.'

(Some scholars think that Mark 2.20 cannot go back to Jesus because it speaks of his death. But does not a time come at every wedding when the bridegroom must leave? Why should not Jesus, who knew himself to be the Servant Messiah, have thus hinted at his death? Verse 20 may well echo Isa. 53.8 where, in the LXX, the verb *airetai*, 'taken away', is used.)

The parables so far surveyed tell of the Kingdom's coming, growth, victorious progress and joy. But, as yet, the authentic note of the Gospel—God's mercy to sinners—has not been heard. The next group of parables will repair that lack.[1]

---

[1] We have said nothing in this chapter about the 'explanations' appended to The Sower, The Tares and The Dragnet, because we believe them to be early Christian expositions. We judge that Jesus did not need to interpret his parables. 'The speaker who needs to interpret his parables is not master of his method,' said A. T. Cadoux. And Jesus was a master.

The full reasons for this view will be found in Jeremias and Dodd. That the 'explanations' allegorize the parables is only one ground, and perhaps not the decisive one. There are two others. (1) The interpretations appended to The Tares and The Dragnet are, as Jeremias shows, studded with 'Mattheanisms'; and the Sower explanation reveals a vocabulary strongly reminiscent of the early Church. (2) The explanations seem to miss the central thrusts of the parables. For example: in the case of The Tares, the main point of the parable (a warning against weeding) disappears in the interpretation which focuses wholly on the Last Judgment.

4

THE GRACE OF THE KINGDOM

THE PARABLES now to be studied lead us to the very heart of the Gospel.

The royalest truth about the Kingdom is that its King is a Father and that his Rule is one of grace—the free love of God to undeserving men. So, in one parable after another, from The Good Employer (which we call The Labourers in the Vineyard) to The Gracious Father (which we name The Prodigal Son) the wonderful kindness of God to unworthy men is hinted, urged, asserted in face of the lovelessness and censoriousness of men. But notice three things:

First: behind all these parables lies Jesus' own 'ministry of reconciliation' which earned him the nickname of 'the Sinners' Friend' (Matt. 11.19; Luke 7.34, Q). It was the heart of the apostolic Gospel that Christ's death had reconciled sinners to God: 'God shows his love for us in that while we were yet sinners Christ died for us' (Rom. 5.8). But Christ's life was all of a piece with his death. The death is but the climax of the ministry of reconciliation in which, by word and deed, he mediated God's forgiveness to men. This ministry is the text on which our parables provide the commentary.

Second: although in these parables Jesus advances no open Christological claim—how could he, when he kept his Messiahship a secret?—in one situation after another he acts as God's Representative, comes forward as the Divine Grace incarnate, says in effect: 'It is because God is like this that I act as I do.'

Third: Most of the parables in this chapter were originally answers to criticisms of his ministry made by Scribes and Pharisees—*ripostes*, if you like, but *ripostes* replete with the

51

grace of God. So, in Christ's mouth, the wrath of man is turned to God's praise, and human hard-heartedness made to proclaim Divine grace.

The saying about The Doctor and the Sick (Mark 2.17) may well stand at their head. It was a fine observation of K. L. Schmidt's that every word or act of Jesus contains the Gospel in miniature. No saying better illustrates it than this one. When the Scribes asked why he consorted with 'publicans and sinners'—with notoriously bad men and women and folk who followed dishonourable or immoral professions[1]—Jesus replied: 'It is not the healthy who need the doctor but the sick (Don't you understand why I gather these outcasts into my company? They are ill and need help!). For I did not come', he adds in one of those sayings in which the secret of his presence in the world is disclosed, 'to call righteous men but sinners.'

Now let us study six parables—two from Matthew, four from Luke—all of which, in one way or another, concern Scribes and Pharisees, vindicate Jesus' ministry among the outcasts, and proclaim the wideness of God's mercy.

We shall begin with The Labourers in the Vineyard, not only because it is one of the most beautiful—and disconcerting—of all the parables but because it most arrestingly proclaims the grace of the God who brings the Kingdom, which is the theme of this chapter. Think of grace, said D. S. Cairns once, as 'the extravagant goodness of God'. The parable invites the Scribes and Pharisees to do just this:

For the kingdom of heaven is like a householder who went out early in the morning to hire labourers for his vineyard.

After agreeing with the labourers for a denarius a day, he sent them into his vineyard. And going out about the third hour he saw others standing idle in the market place; and to them he said, 'You go into the vineyard too, and whatever is right I will give

---

[1] 'Sinners' means (a) people who led an immoral life, e.g. adulterers and swindlers (Luke 18.11) and (b) people who followed a profession which involved dishonesty or immorality (tax-collectors, donkey-drivers, pedlars and even shepherds!) and so lost their civil rights. See Jeremias, op. cit., 132.

you.' So they went. Going out again about the sixth hour and the ninth hour he did the same. And about the eleventh hour he went out and found others standing, and he said to them, 'Why do you stand here idle all day?' They said to him, 'Because no one has hired us.' He said to them, 'You go into the vineyard too.'

And when evening came, the owner of the vineyard said to his steward, 'Call the labourers and pay them their wages, beginning with the last, up to the first.' And when those hired about the eleventh hour came, each of them received a denarius. Now when the first came, they thought they would receive more; but each of them also received a denarius. And on receiving it they grumbled at the householder, saying, 'These last worked only one hour, and you have made them equal to us who have borne the burden of the day and the scorching heat.'

But he replied to one of them, 'Friend, I am doing you no wrong; did you not agree with me for a denarius? Take what belongs to you, and go; I choose to give to this last as I give to you. Am I not allowed to do what I choose with what belongs to me? Or do you begrudge my generosity?' (Matt. 20.1-15).

This parable excellently illustrates the 'rule of end stress', for the spotlight falls on the employer's astonishing generosity to the eleventh hour labourers which provokes the indignant protest of those who had worked the whole day. But the employer will have none of it: 'Friend, I'm not swindling you', he says, 'You are getting what we agreed on. Must I be mean to these unfortunates because you are envious?'

By the eleventh hour labourers Jesus undoubtedly meant the publicans and sinners who were answering his call to God's Kingdom. Equally certain is it that the protesters were the Scribes and Pharisees who imagined that their special merits entitled them to special rewards from God. And the parable exposes their protest as a selfish concern for their own deserts. The rewards of the Kingdom (it says) are not to be measured by man's deserts but by God's grace. 'God', says Jesus to them, 'is like this kind employer. His goodness gives according to our needs and not according to our deserts. Even to undeserving sinners he grants a place in his Kingdom. And because God is like this, I act as I do.'

This parable will always offend those who want to apply to it the rules of strict justice or of sound economics. To such people the only reply is (as T. W. Manson says)[1] that 'it is fortunate for most of us that God does not deal with us on the basis of strict justice and sound economics. In the last resort the rewards of such poor service as men can give to the Kingdom are not an exact *quid pro quo*. They are an expression of God's love towards his servants; and God's love cannot be portioned out in quantities nicely adjusted to the merits of individuals. There is such a thing as a twelfth part of a denar. It was called a *pondion*. But there is no such thing as a twelfth part of the love of God.'

Grace has been defined as 'the love of God, spontaneous, beautiful, unearned, at work in Jesus Christ for the salvation of men'. This is the theology of the parable—and of the Gospel.

Perhaps this parable was Jesus' answer to the complaint that he opened God's Kingdom to publicans and prostitutes, which is the theme of The Two Sons. Once again, we have a rebuke of the Scribes and Pharisees. 'They say and do not', was Jesus' verdict on them (Matt. 23.3), whereas he found that so-called reprobates like tax-gatherers and harlots, who made no pious claims, had a way of closing with God's call when it came to them. Jesus' parable convicts the Scribes and Pharisees out of their own mouth. The tale is about two sons whom their father sent to work in his vineyard, and it needs no great penetration to see that the first son represents the publicans and harlots, the second the Scribes and Pharisees:

What do you think? A man had two sons, and he went to the first and said, 'Son, go and work in the vineyard today.' And he answered, 'I will not'; but afterward he repented and went. And he went to the second son and said the same; and he answered, 'I go, sir'; but did not go. Which of the two did the will of his father? They said, 'The first.' Jesus said to them, 'Truly I say to you, the tax collectors and the harlots go into the kingdom of God before you' (Matt. 21.28-31).

Invited to pass judgment on a simple story, the Scribes and Pharisees find, like King David, that 'the story pops up and

[1] *The Sayings of Jesus*, 220.

leaves them flat'. For before they quite know what they are saying, they are admitting that penitent publicans and prostitutes are nearer to God's grace than professing churchmen who ignore his call.

Alongside The Two Sons we may set the parable of The Two Debtors, which has much in common with it (the number two, Pharisees and prostitutes). It comes to us embedded in the tale of the sinful woman—no doubt a woman of the streets—who anointed Jesus' feet in Simon the Pharisee's house (Luke 7.36-50). Her quite extraordinary display of gratitude[1] compels us to assume that Jesus had previously assured her of God's forgiveness as only he could. But Simon can only see in her a 'bad woman'. So Jesus tells him a story:

A certain creditor had two debtors; one owed five hundred denarii, and the other fifty. When they could not pay, he forgave them both. Now which of them will love him more? Simon answered, 'The one, I suppose, to whom he forgave more.' And he said to him, 'You have judged rightly' (Luke 7.41-43).

What Jesus is saying is something like this: 'Isn't it the person who has had the greater debts remitted who shows the greater gratitude (lit. "will love more")?'[2] Simon is forced to agree. Then Jesus says, 'I tell you, Simon, God must have remitted very great spiritual debts for her, since she shows so much gratitude.'

If The Two Sons says to the Scribes and Pharisees, 'The taxgatherers and harlots are going into the Kingdom before you', The Two Debtors says to an individual Pharisee, 'This "bad woman" is nearer to God than you are.'

We may now take two parables from Luke 14, The Great Supper and Places at Table.

That The Great Supper in Luke and The Marriage Feast in Matthew (Matt. 22.1-10) are different versions of the same

---

[1] Luke 7.38 'What an extraordinary demonstration! we are tempted to say. Was it hysterics, the weakness of a breaking wave? No, it was not hysterics, it was regeneration.' Denney, *The Christian Doctrine of Reconciliation*, 14.

[2] See Jeremias, op. cit., 127.

parable, no reputable scholar nowadays denies. Just as little does anyone doubt that Luke preserves it more faithfully.[1]

In Luke's Gospel the parable is introduced—and the connexion is too apt to be mere editor's work—by the story of a man who one day said to Jesus at table, 'Blessed is he who shall eat bread in the kingdom of God!' It was the kind of pious platitude calculated to evoke from Jesus a crisp rejoinder. We may imagine a few moments of grim silence; then Jesus said, 'Let me tell you a story:

A man once gave a great banquet, and invited many; and at the time for the banquet he sent his servant to say to those who had been invited, "Come; for all is now ready." But they all alike began to make excuses. The first said to him, "I have bought a field, and I must go out and see it; I pray you, have me excused." And another said, "I have bought five yoke of oxen, and I go to examine them; I pray you, have me excused." And another said, "I have married a wife, and therefore I cannot come." So the servant came and reported this to his master. Then the householder in anger said to his servant, "Go out quickly to the streets and lanes of the city, and bring in the poor and maimed and blind and lame." And the servant said, "Sir, what you commanded has been done, and still there is room." And the master said to his servant, "Go out to the highways and hedges, and compel people to come in, that my house may be filled. For I tell you, none of those men who were invited shall taste my banquet" ' (Luke 14.16-24).

It is a tale—not without allegorical features—of how guests invited to a great banquet excused themselves at the last moment and then found their places filled by people from off the streets and the highways.

That the banquet, which stands 'ready', means the Kingdom

---

[1] Matthew's account has suffered in transmission. Luke's 'supper' has become a 'marriage feast' which a 'king' (God) makes for his 'son' (Christ). Verses 6-7 interrupt the story and are clearly a reference to the destruction of Jerusalem in AD 70, seen as God's act of vengeance on Israel for the maltreatment of his servants. In verses 11-13 we have a separate parable, The Man without the Wedding Garment, which has been tacked on, presumably because Matthew—or his source—thought that the parable made salvation too easy for the sinner and therefore insisted on the need for a robe of righteousness (or repentance). Finally, right at the end comes an aphorism, 'Many are called but few are chosen,' which fits neither 2-10 nor 11-13, though it may none the less be an authentic saying of Jesus.

of God is clear. The double invitation—an earlier general one and a later 'bidding' at the actual time—accords with Oriental custom. If, as seems likely, the 'servant' is a veiled reference to Jesus himself, we have here a genuine allegorical feature, and we may then think of the guests as signifying his own people whom the prophets had prepared for his coming. (In verses 21 ff. the allegorical nature of the parable is indisputable, since householders who order their houses to be filled at all costs simply don't exist on earth! The reference here is undoubtedly to God.) When the original guests decline, making various 'cares of this world' their excuses, the servant is dispatched to invite, first, men from the city streets and lanes and then, when there is still room, men from the highways and hedges. Once again, it is hard to avoid the conclusion that Jesus is thinking of 'sinners' and Gentiles.[1]

The parable, then, is a warning against self-deception addressed to the professedly religious in the land of whom his pious table companion was type. 'Ah, what happiness it will be (you say) to get an invitation to God's banquet and accept it! But this is precisely the chance you have been offered, and see what you have done with your invitation! And if God now proposes to find places at table for sinners and Gentiles, you have only yourselves to blame. It is not God who has excluded you; you have excluded yourselves.'

We might rename it the parable of The Contemptuous Guests; and its moral, which is still valid, is that if God invites men into his Kingdom, their salvation depends on their accepting his invitation.

When Luke included the parable about Places at Table in the same general context as The Great Supper, he obviously believed they had a common theme. As indeed they have, if our interpretation is correct. The first one says: 'If you find yourselves outside the Kingdom of God, you have only yourselves to blame.' The second warns: 'You are making a big

[1] We are entitled to regard this mission to 'the highways and the hedges' in Luke 14.23 as a secondary feature only if we can show that Jesus never envisaged a Gentile mission. Cf. Mark 11.17.

mistake if you think you can pick the best places for yourselves in the Kingdom.'

Now he told a parable to those who were invited, when he marked how they chose the places of honour, saying to them,
'When you are invited by any one to a marriage feast, do not sit down in a place of honour, lest a more eminent man than you be invited by him; and he who invited you both will come and say to you, "Give place to this man," and then you will begin with shame to take the lowest place. But when you are invited, go and sit in the lowest place, so that when your host comes he may say to you, "Friend, go up higher"; then you will be honoured in the presence of all who sit at table with you. For every one who exalts himself will be humbled, and he who humbles himself will be exalted' (Luke 14.7-11).

Prima facie, this reads like a picturesque way of saying, 'It pays to be modest'; and not a new saying either, since the gist of it occurs in Prov. 25.6 f., and a later rabbi called Simeon b.Zakkai is credited with giving similar advice. Was Jesus simply repeating an old rule of etiquette?

Luke however calls it a 'parable', i.e. something which argues from human relations to divine; and the probability is that what Jesus did was to turn this familiar piece of etiquette into a parable of the Kingdom.

It was uttered during some table-talk between Jesus and the Pharisees when he could not help observing their inordinate fondness for the chief places. On the spiritual level, this represents what we might call the 'V.I.P.' mentality which makes a man think himself God's favourite and therefore entitled to preferential treatment in his Kingdom. It is this 'Diotrephic'[1] temper which the parable rebukes.

Self-honour (it says) is no honour. The only honour worthy the name is that given you by another. So it is in God's Realm. God honours those who presume no title to his favour. In Kingdom terms: 'The best places are in God's gift and not in man's choice. Better not try to make up God's mind for him, or you may get an unpleasant surprise!'

[1] 'Diotrephes, who loveth to have the pre-eminence among them' (III John 9).

It is a spiritual axiom with Jesus that none are so far from God as the self-righteous. This is what he is saying in the parable of The Pharisee and the Publican:

Two men went up into the temple to pray, one a Pharisee and the other a tax collector. The Pharisee stood and prayed thus with himself, 'God, I thank thee that I am not like other men, extortioners, unjust, adulterers or even like this tax collector. I fast twice a week, I give tithes of all that I get.' But the tax collector, standing afar off, would not even lift up his eyes to heaven, but beat his breast, saying, 'God, be merciful to me a sinner!' I tell you, this man went down to his house justified rather than the other (Luke 18.10-14a).

First comes the vivid picture of the two men in the Temple: the one 'standing by himself', reminding God of his religious achievements, and even using the tax collector as 'a dark foil for his own gleaming whiteness'; the other, 'standing far off', with his eyes on the ground, and so overwhelmed by his own unworthiness that all he can say is, 'God, be merciful to me a sinner!' But how startling to the Pharisees who heard it must have been Jesus' verdict on the two men: 'God has justified the one, not the other'.[1] 'Justified' suggests Paul's teaching about justification, and this is precisely the parable's theme. 'It is the beggars before God who are blessed', said Jesus in the First Beatitude (Matt. 5.3). This is the Beatitude made into a parable.[2]

But it is in the three parables of the Lost (Luke 15), all of them replies to the criticism of the Scribes and Pharisees, that God's grace to sinners is supremely proclaimed.

The parable of The Lost Sheep (possibly drawn from Q) is made in Matthew 18.12-14 to teach God's concern for backsliding 'brethren' in the Christian fellowship. But who can doubt that Luke is right in regarding it as Jesus' vindication, against the Pharisees, of his mission to sinners?

[1] For the translation see Jeremias, op. cit., 141. Behind the Greek word rendered 'rather than' lies an Aramaic *min* used with exclusive force. Gen. 38.26 in Hebrew and Greek is a splendid parallel. 'Tamar is righteous, I am not.'

[2] Luke 18.8b is a saying from another context which has the effect of making the parable a general lesson in humility.

What man of you, having a hundred sheep, if he has lost one of them, does not leave the ninety-nine in the wilderness, and go after the one which is lost, until he finds it? And when he has found it, he lays it on his shoulders, rejoicing. And when he comes home, he calls together his friends and neighbours, saying to them, 'Rejoice with me, for I have found my sheep which was lost.' Even so I tell you there will be more joy in heaven over one sinner who repents than over ninety-nine righteous persons who need no repentance (Luke 15.4-7).

It is a parable of the redemptive joy of God. 'I tell you', said Jesus to his critics, 'that in the same way God rejoices more over one sinner who repents than over ninety-nine respectable persons who have never committed any gross sin.'[1]

If The Lost Coin was originally its 'twin', as seems likely, we may guess that it was meant to appeal to women, as the other to men:

Or what woman, having ten silver coins, if she loses one coin, does not light a lamp and sweep the house and seek diligently until she finds it? And when she has found it, she calls together her friends and neighbours, saying, 'Rejoice with me, for I have found the coin which I had lost.' Even so, I tell you, there is joy before the angels of God over one sinner who repents (Luke 15.8-10).

The point is the same: 'If a woman shows such joy over the recovery of a lost piece of property (was the coin a bit of her headdress and part of her dowry?), how much more does God when he recovers a lost child! This is why I seek out sinners and welcome them.'

The third in the series of the Lost—The Prodigal Son—is, by common consent, the paragon of all parables:

There was a man who had two sons; and the younger of them said to his father, 'Father, give me the share of property that falls to me.' And he divided his living between them. Not many days later, the younger son gathered all he had and took his journey into a far country, and there he squandered his property in loose living. And when he had spent everything, a great famine arose in that country, and he began to be in want. So he went and joined himself to one of the citizens of that country, who sent him into

[1] For the translation see Jeremias, op. cit., 135. On the 'newness' of the idea of 'the seeking God', see Montefiore, *The Synoptic Gospels*, II, 520.

his fields to feed swine. And he would gladly have fed on the pods that the swine ate; and no one gave him anything. But when he came to himself he said, 'How many of my father's hired servants have bread enough and to spare, but I perish here with hunger! I will arise and go to my father, and I will say to him, Father, I have sinned against heaven and before you; I am no longer worthy to be called your son; treat me as one of your hired servants.' And he arose and came to his father. But while he was yet at a distance, his father saw him and had compassion, and ran and embraced him and kissed him. And the son said to him, 'Father, I have sinned against heaven and before you; I am no longer worthy to be called your son.' But the father said to his servants, 'Bring quickly the best robe and put it on him; and put a ring on his hand, and shoes on his feet; and bring the fatted calf and kill it, and let us eat and make merry; for this my son was dead, and is alive again; he was lost, and is found.' And they began to make merry.

Now his elder son was in the field; and as he came and drew near to the house, he heard music and dancing. And he called one of the servants and asked what this meant. And he said to him, 'Your brother has come, and your father has killed the fatted calf, because he has received him safe and sound.' But he was angry and refused to go in. His father came out and entreated him, but he answered his father, 'Lo, these many years I have served you, and I never disobeyed your command; yet you never gave me a kid, that I might make merry with my friends. But when this son of yours came, who has devoured your living with harlots, you killed for him the fatted calf!' And he said to him, 'Son, you are always with me, and all that is mine is yours. It was fitting to make merry and be glad, for this your brother was dead, and is alive; he was lost, and is found' (Luke 15.11-32).

How consummately the tale is told! No wonder Robert Bridges, a fastidious critic, pronounced it 'an absolutely flawless piece of work'. Yet its artistry should not make us forget that it originated in Jesus' 'warfare' with the Pharisees. But if it is polemic, it is polemic at its finest, polemic armed with the gentleness of love.

The story, with its deep psychological insights and its wonderful 'anatomy of repentance', is too life-like to be called an allegory. Yet, beyond doubt, in the mind of Jesus the father stood for God, the elder brother for the Scribes and Pharisees, and the prodigal for publicans and sinners.

It is important to realize that this is one of his two-pointed parables. We should therefore reject all suggestions that it might have ended at verse 24 ('For this my son was dead', etc.).[1] The second half of the story is not an appendix which we may include or omit at will. It makes a point at least as important as the first half. Indeed, we may say that the contrast on which the whole parable hinges is that of the attitudes of the father and of the elder brother to the prodigal.

Observe how masterfully Jesus works it out. First, he forces his hearers to pronounce a judgment on the way in which the Prodigal is treated, first by the father, and then by his brother. He compels them to admit that the father's way is as wholly right as the brother's is wrong. But, once this judgment is made, equally compelling is the transfer of the whole issue to the spiritual sphere: 'If you condemn the attitude of the Elder Brother, you must likewise condemn the attitude of Scribes and Pharisees to sinners. You must admit that it is only when a penitent sinner is treated as a son that he has any hope of becoming one.'

In the parable, then, Jesus does two things. To begin with, he justifies his own mission in the teeth of his critics: 'God is like the father of my story. This is his way with sinners, and therefore it is my way.' But, secondly, he rebukes the Scribes and Pharisees: 'You represent the Elder Brother in my story, because your way of treating sinners is his. But it is the wrong way, because it is not God's way.' A rebuke, then, but a rebuke instinct with love: 'Son, you are always with me, and all that is mine is yours. It was fitting to make merry and be glad, for this your brother was dead, and is alive; he was lost and is

---

[1] The unity of the parable is expressed in the opening verse: 'A certain man had *two* sons.' And it is really the tale of *two lost* sons; for the elder brother was a prodigal too—in that he was completely out of harmony with his father's way of life—even if, physically, he had never left home.

The trouble is that when we are in the condition of the prodigal, we recognize ourselves readily enough; whereas when we are in the condition of the elder brother—which is equally sad—we are much less willing to admit the resemblance.

found.' The rebuke turns into an appeal—the appeal of love for love.

Of course the parable does not give us a complete exposition of God's nature. No parable does. Therefore we have no right to fault it because it makes no reference to the atoning death of Christ whereby sinners are reconciled to God. All that Jesus does in the parable—and how much it is—is to state the fundamental principle of God's dealings with sinners, and thereby justify his own loving concern for them. What we are entitled to learn from the parable is that God loves the sinner before he repents, and that, when he does, God forgives him and restores him to his great family. Over the whole parable, as sub-title, might be inscribed Paul's words, 'God who justifies the ungodly'. This was the heart of Paul's theology, but it was the Lord's, before it was Paul's.[1]

[1] In *Agape and Eros*, 82 f., Nygren acutely criticizes Jülicher's treatment of The Prodigal Son.

According to Jülicher, Jesus' parables, employing simple analogies from life, compelled his hearers to admit as 'self-evident' similar truth in the spiritual realm. This sounds fair enough until Jülicher cites The Prodigal Son as a good example. The hearer (says Jülicher) has to own that 'it actually happens so in the world', and since an earthly father would so act, so does the Heavenly Father.

But this (says Nygren) is to misunderstand the parable. On Jülicher's view, the parable is not self-evident, and as a proof from human life it is quite unconvincing. Why? Because an opponent, on appeal being made to human life, could easily have described *another* father who, knowing the value of a wastrel's fine professions, ordered the returning prodigal first to make good his penitence by honest work. The son did so, and, his probation over, thanked his father for the severity that led to his amendment. Now, the opponent of Jesus might well claim that this is how 'it actually happens in life' and go on to claim that the Heavenly Father acts likewise. In short, the love of the Father in this parable is the love not of an ordinary but of an extraordinary father. It is a sheer grace for the undeserving that Jesus describes. It is the God who freely forgives the man who has no claim on his forgiveness.

We can supply Bishop Nygren with an even better illustration of his point. The story is told of a certain prodigal son who, on turning up in 'the far country' of another parish, was advised by the minister there to go home and 'his father would kill the fatted calf for him'. The prodigal obeyed; and, months after, meeting the same minister again, was asked, hopefully: 'Well, and did he kill the fatted calf for you?' 'No,' came the rueful reply, 'but he nearly killed the prodigal son!'

Who will deny that it has often happened so in real life?

5

THE MEN OF THE KINGDOM

B Y N O means all the parables were *ripostes* to criticism: many were spurs to perception.

When Abraham Lincoln found it necessary, in dealing with the men around him, to drive home a difficult—or disagreeable—truth, he would often do it by means of a homely story. The Gospel reveals Jesus doing the same thing, in parable after parable. Before we study them, one important point needs making.

Read the Gospels carefully, and you cannot escape the conclusion that where Jesus is, there is the Kingdom. *Ubi Christus* (we may say), *ibi Regnum Dei*. He embodies God's Rule. Origen was to sum it up in one word, *autobasileia*: Jesus himself is the Kingdom. And therefore to attach oneself to Jesus as his disciple is to become a Kingdom man—a son of the Kingdom. What kind of men are required for the Kingdom? A dozen or more parables supply the answer.

It was to confront men with the Kingdom's claims that Jesus spoke the twin parables of The Hid Treasure and The Costly Pearl. We have them now only in outline—how graphic they must have been in the first telling!

The kingdom of heaven is like treasure hidden in a field, which a man found and covered up; then in his joy he goes and sells all that he has and buys that field.

Again, the kingdom of heaven is like a merchant in search of fine pearls, who, on finding one pearl of great value, went and sold all that he had and bought it (Matt. 13.44-46).

Both parables challenge to decision: 'The Kingdom is wealth which demonetizes all other currencies.[1] Are you ready

[1] T. W. Manson, *The Sayings of Jesus*, 196.

64

to part with all in order to gain it?' In The Hid Treasure, observe, the man stumbles on his wealth, whereas in The Costly Pearl he finds it only after long searching. Surely this reveals Jesus' awareness that it is often by very different roads that men come to the Kingdom, as all Christian history attests. (If one man's road lay by the toll house in Capernaum, another's began in Tarsus, wound round the school of Gamaliel in Jerusalem, and only ended on a desert track near Damascus.)

But Jesus will have no rash disciples. Solemnly he warns all such to heed well the consequences. This is the *caveat* contained in the two parables of The Tower Builder and The Warring King, which probably come from the height of the Galilean Ministry when many were offering to follow him (Luke 9.57-62):

For which of you, desiring to build a tower, does not first sit down and count the cost, whether he has enough to complete it? Otherwise, when he has laid a foundation, and is not able to finish, all who see it begin to mock him, saying, 'This man began to build, and was not able to finish.'

Or what king, going to encounter another king in war, will not sit down first and take counsel whether he is able with ten thousand to meet him who comes against him with twenty thousand? And if not, while the other is yet a great way off, he sends an embassy and asks terms of peace (Luke 14.28-32).

In the first parable Jesus says, 'Sit down and reckon whether you can afford to follow me.' In the second he says: 'Sit down and reckon whether you can afford to refuse my demands.'

He does not seek to scare men from following him, but he does call for complete commitment. They must, in cold blood, count all that discipleship will mean in loss of family ties, a new world of values, a hard and uncertain future, with, liker than not, a cross at the end of the road.

Despite Jesus' strictures on the Scribes, we know that at least one of them would fain have followed him (Matt 8.19). Perhaps the little parable of The Householder was his answer to a Scribe who had volunteered his allegiance but wondered

3

whether what he had learned 'under the Law' would be useless in the high emprise of the Kingdom:

Every scribe who has been trained for the kingdom of heaven is like a householder who brings out of his treasure what is new and what is old (Matt. 13.52).

A Scribe who becomes my disciple, says Jesus, will be able to wed the wisdoms of the Old Order to the truths of the New.

What qualities does Jesus desiderate in disciples? The will to serve God selflessly is one of them, as we might expect in those called to follow One who knew himself to be the Servant Messiah. Disciples must recognize that they are, first and foremost, servants of God summoned to unreserved obedience. This is the point of the dry little story of The Farmer and His Man:

Will any one of you, who has a servant ploughing or keeping sheep, say to him when he has come in from the field, 'Come at once and sit down at table?' Will he not rather say to him, 'Prepare supper for me, and gird yourself and serve me, till I eat and drink; and afterward you shall eat and drink'? Does he thank the servant because he did what was commanded? So you also, when you have done all that is commanded you, say, 'We are unworthy servants; we have only done what was our duty' (Luke 17.7-10).

Doubtless when it was first spoken, this story carried a warning against the Pharisees' legalist preoccupation with 'merit'. 'You never find a farmer', says Jesus in effect, 'fussing over a servant because he has done a hard day's work and carried out his orders. So you, as God's servants, must obey him without thought of reward.'

Of course this is not a denial that God rewards his faithful servants. 'Jesus', as Bultmann says finely, 'promises reward to those who are obedient without thought of reward.' And the best evidence is his promise, in the Last Judgment scene (Matt. 25.31-46), of God's benediction on those who have selflessly succoured all his hungry, unfriended and sick children.

A second quality demanded of the disciple is practical prudence, shrewdness, 'savvy'—all, in short, that we mean by that wonderful word 'gumption'.[1]

Once, in sending the disciples out on their mission, Jesus bade them be 'wise as serpents and harmless as doves' (Matt. 10.16); and in the story of The Unjust Steward it is just this wisdom that he requires of them:

There was a rich man who had a steward, and charges were brought to him that this man was wasting his goods. And he called him and said to him, 'What is this I hear about you? Turn in the account of your stewardship, for you can no longer be steward.' And the steward said to himself, 'What shall I do, since my master is taking the stewardship away from me? I am not strong enough to dig, and I am ashamed to beg. I have decided what to do, so that people may receive me into their houses when I am put out of the stewardship.' So, summoning his master's debtors one by one, he said to the first, 'How much do you owe my master?' He said, 'A hundred measures of oil.' And he said to him, 'Take your bill, and sit down quickly and write fifty.' Then he said to another, 'And how much do you owe?' He said, 'A hundred measures of wheat.' He said to him, 'Take your bill, and write eighty.' The master commended the dishonest steward for his prudence; for the sons of this world are wiser in their own generation than the sons of light (Luke 16.1-8).

Here is an estate manager—what we call in Scotland a 'factor'—who, when he mismanaged his master's affairs and was dismissed, quickly realized that, in his situation, friendship meant more to him than hard cash and shrewdly secured his own future. We need not go into details. But notice its ending: 'And the Lord (*kyrios*) praised the unjust steward because he had acted wisely, for the sons of this world are wiser in their own generation than the sons of light.'

We take 'the Lord' to be Jesus, not the steward's master (Cf. Luke 16.8). What Jesus applauded was not the man's roguery but his resourcefulness in a tight spot. A rascal but a clever one! And Jesus is saying in effect: 'Give me men who will

[1] Professor ('Rabbi') Duncan of New College, Edinburgh, addressing the departing students, is reported to have said: 'What you need, gentlemen, are the three Gs—Greek, Grace and Gumption. If you haven't Greek, you can learn it. If you haven't Grace, you can pray for it. But if you haven't Gumption, the Lord help you!'

show as much practical sense in God's business as worldlings do in theirs.'

But spiritual *savoir faire* is not enough. The sons of the Kingdom should possess strong faith, a forgiving spirit and unlimited love.

Oligopistoi, 'Little-faiths', he called the disciples (Matt. 6.30; 8.26; 14.31; 16.8), rallying them tenderly; and three parables have survived (there must have been more) to tell us how he strove to make them trust God more.

The first has been called The Asking Son (Matt 7.9-11; Luke 11.11-13, Q). A comparison of the passages in Matthew and Luke reveals that for Matthew's 'loaf' and 'stone' Luke has 'egg' and 'scorpion'. Since bread, fish and eggs were the three staple foods of Palestine, it is likely that Jesus referred to all three, as some MSS. of Luke declare:

> What man of you, if his son asks him for a loaf, will give him a stone?
> Or if he asks for a fish, will give him a serpent?
> Or if he asks for an egg, will give him a scorpion?
> If you then, who are evil, know how to give good gifts to your children, how much more will your Father who is in heaven give good things to those who ask him?

The argument is: 'No ordinary human father—and the best of them are far from perfect—would play a scurvy trick like this on his son. How much less, then, the good Father above!' We cannot imagine our Lord using the lawyers' language about 'acts of God'; the royal language about 'acts of grace' would have been very much more to his mind.

The second parable of faith is commonly called The Friend at Midnight, though it might be better named 'The Churlish Householder':

> Which of you who has a friend will go to him at midnight and say to him, 'Friend, lend me three loaves; for a friend of mine has arrived on a journey, and I have nothing to set before him'; and he will answer from within, 'Do not bother me; the door is now shut, and my children are with me in bed; I cannot get up and give you anything?' I tell you, though he will not get up and give

him anything because he is his friend, yet because of his importunity he will rise and give him whatever he needs (Luke 11.5-8).

It is a simple village story. Here is a man who at midnight knocks up his neighbour, sleeping among his children,[1] and asks for three loaves to feed an unexpected guest. In the end he gets them, but only after much knocking. Knocking suggests prayer; but the point can hardly be simply the need for sheer persistence in it, as though Jesus believed God must give way before this barrage of prayer—men are not heard, he said, merely for their 'much speaking' (Matt. 6.7). The parable is meant to stimulate not so much perseverance in prayer as faith that their prayers will be answered. 'If even a man with so many reasons for being disobliging', runs the argument, 'can be moved to give you what you ask, how much more will God lend a ready ear to his children's requests.'

The companion parable to this is The Importunate Widow (though, since he is the chief character, it might better be called 'The Unconscionable Judge'):

In a certain city there was a judge who neither feared God nor regarded man; and there was a widow in that city who kept coming to him and saying, 'Vindicate me against my adversary.' For a while he refused; but afterward he said to himself, 'Though I neither fear God nor regard man, yet because this widow bothers me, I will vindicate her, or she will wear me out by her continual coming.' And the Lord said, 'Hear what the unrighteous judge says. And will not God vindicate his elect, who cry to him day and night? Will he delay long over them? I tell you, he will vindicate them speedily' (Luke 18.2-8a).[2]

Need we say that Jesus is not describing some dourly ungracious Deity who requires to be badgered into compliance? As in the previous parable, the argument is 'by contraries'. If even this unprincipled judge could be moved by the widow's

---

[1] 'The children sleep in a row, sized like a shepherd's pan pipes, and the parents one at each end of the row, all sleeping on the floor. And you do not lightly rise to pick your way across the sleeping company.' J. M. C. Crum, *The Original Jerusalem Gospel*, 54.

[2] Luke 18.8b is secondary. Apart from its unusual question-form, it bears traces of Luke's own style, and it ill consists with the mood of the parable.

importunity into action, how much more will God answer his people's prayers for vindication! Indeed, the parable reads like a comment on the Fourth Beautitude, 'Blessed are those who hunger and thirst for righteousness (i.e. who ardently desire to see God putting things right),[1] for they shall be satisfied' (Matt. 5.6).

Such are the parables of faith. We are bound to add that Jesus himself was the 'pioneer and perfecter' of it. How shall we explain his miracles? 'Answers to his prayers', answers D. S. Cairns, 'works of his own faith in God and of the Divine Spirit in answer to the appeal of his faith.'[2] And Jesus was convinced that even his disciples, if they had something of his own perfect faith, might similarly 'expect great things from God'.

At the heart of the Gospel of the Kingdom lies the assurance of the Divine forgiveness, a forgiveness which Jesus, appearing as the Divine pardon incarnate, mediated to sinful men and women. Freely they had received, and Jesus expected them in turn freely to forgive. 'Be merciful', he said, 'as your Father is merciful' (Luke 6.36).

St Matthew has preserved one parable in which this point is trenchantly driven home. It is the story of The Unmerciful Servant:

The kingdom of heaven may be compared to a king who wished to settle accounts with his servants. When he began the reckoning, one was brought to him who owed him ten thousand talents; and as he could not pay, his lord ordered him to be sold, with his wife and children and all that he had, and payment to be made. So the servant fell on his knees, imploring him, 'Lord, have patience with me, and I will pay you everything.' And out of pity for him the lord of that servant released him and forgave him the debt. But that same servant, as he went out, came upon one of his fellow servants, who owed him a hundred denarii; and seizing him by the throat, he said, 'Pay what you owe.' So his fellow servant fell down and besought him, 'Have patience with me, and I will pay you.' He refused and went and put him in prison till he should pay the debt. When his fellow servants saw what had taken place,

---

[1] For the translation see my *Design for life*, 33 f.
[2] *David S. Cairns, An Autobiography*, 193.

they were greatly distressed, and went and reported to their lord all that had taken place. Then his lord summoned him and said to him, 'You wicked servant! I forgave you all that debt, because you besought me, and should not you have had mercy on your fellow servant, as I had mercy on you?' And in anger his lord delivered him to the jailers, till he should pay all his debt. So also my heavenly Father will do to every one of you, if you do not forgive your brother from your heart (Matt. 18.23-35).

By the 'servant' in this tale we are to understand some high-ranking steward in a king's service. When the king, hearing his plea, compassionately forgave him the huge debt he owed him, the steward refused to show a like pity to a fellow servant owing him a paltry sum and had him clapped into prison. Then the jailed man's friends indignantly appealed to the king who, wroth at the steward's ruthlessness, revoked his original pardon.

Such is the story, and its meaning is plain enough. The men of the Kingdom must show to others the forgiveness they have themselves received. He who refuses to forgive a man who has wronged him (and what Jesus demands is not mere lip forgiveness, but forgiveness 'from the heart') must expect God to judge his sins with like severity.

Perhaps it is worth noting the sums of money mentioned in the parable. The steward's debt to the king was some two million pounds; a vast debt which he had no hope of repaying. By contrast, his fellow servant owed him five pounds. May not this be Jesus' way of reminding us that the debt others owe us is but a drop beside the ocean of our indebtedness to God?

The parable is a comment on the Fifth Beatitude, 'Blessed are the merciful, for they shall obtain mercy' (Matt. 5.7).[1]

Forgiveness leads on naturally and inevitably to love. We know that for Jesus the two great principles of love to God and love to neighbour, together with the Golden Rule, super-

[1] Along with this parable should go that of The Mote and The Beam (Matt. 7.3-5; Luke 6.41 f., Q), which is a warning against censoriousness. It is worth noting that the man who tries to remove the 'splinter' from his brother's eye is said to have a 'plank' in his own! It is the same point as in The Unmerciful Servant.

seded all other commandments and formed 'a complete equip-
ment for the adventure of good living'. Once, when a Scribe
agreed about the primacy of love, Jesus declared him to have
the right moral disposition for the Kingdom (Mark 12.28-34);
and probably it was well known that Jesus taught his disciples
to find the essence of true religion in the great twin command.

It was probably in this knowledge that another Scribe, eager
to know the secret of 'eternal life', asked the typical lawyer's
question: 'But where does one draw the line between neighbour and non-neighbour?' Jesus' answer was the parable of
The Good Samaritan:

A man was going down from Jerusalem to Jericho, and he fell
among robbers who stripped him and beat him, and departed
leaving him half-dead. Now by chance a priest was going down
that road; and when he saw him, he passed by on the other side.
So likewise a Levite, when he came to the place, and saw him,
passed by on the other side. But a Samaritan, as he journeyed,
came to where he was; and when he saw him, he had compassion,
and went to him and bound up his wounds, pouring on oil and
wine; then he set him on his own beast and brought him to an
inn, and took care of him. And the next day he took out two
denarii, and gave them to the innkeeper, saying, 'Take care of
him, and whatever more you spend, I will repay you when I come
back.'
Which of these three, do you think, proved neighbour to the
man who fell among the robbers? He said, 'The one who showed
mercy on him.' And Jesus said to him, 'Go and do likewise' (Luke
10.30-37).

It has been complained that Jesus did not answer the lawyer's question, 'Who is my neighbour?' Let those who will
make this cavil, for the truth is that the lawyer's question is
unanswerable. Real love—*agape* as Jesus understands it—does
not ask for limits but only for opportunity; and when a man
has *agape* in his heart, he will never ask the Scribe's question.

But in fact Jesus did answer the question, though not in the
Scribe's terms. 'Anyone in need', he said, 'is your neighbour.'
For, as in the case of The Prodigal Son, this parable has some-
thing of love's polemic about it. No doubt when Jesus men-

tioned the priest and the Levite,[1] he was thinking of the churchmen and theologians of his day; and what he says in the parable is something like this: 'Here, by your own admission, is a half-breed heretic fulfilling God's law better than the pillars of Jewry. This is what neighbour-love means, my friend, and if you want eternal life, this is the kind of action God requires of you.'

The parables we have reviewed show how the sons of the Kingdom ought to live. But for Jesus his disciple-band formed the nucleus of the New Israel which had served itself heir to the tasks left unfulfilled by the Old. How did he conceive of their role in the world?

In the next chapter we shall consider the parable of The Savourless Salt, because it was originally directed at Old Israel. Judaism had become like 'insipid salt'. But, by implication, it tells us how Jesus thought of the mission of the New Israel. 'Your task is to do what good salt does, to preserve—to preserve the world from corruption.'

So with the parable of The Lamp and the Bushel. The Scribes had hidden the light of God's revelation—the *Torah*—under a meal-tub, so that it could no longer give light. But a lighted lamp should stand where its beam will show to all—on the lampstand. So the New Israel is called to be 'the light of the world' (Matt. 5.14; cf. Isa. 42.6).

The saying about The City set on a Hill (Matt. 5.14) may well be more fully preserved in the version found at Oxyrhynchus:

'A city built on a hilltop cannot be overthrown or hidden.' Impregnability and visibility are the main ideas. It is a word of assurance and challenge to the disciples. A 'little flock of God' they may be (Luke 12.32), but, as citizens of the impregnable City of God (cf. Isa. 2.2-4; Matt. 16.18), they are the cynosure of all eyes and must quit themselves like true servants of the Lord.

---

[1] Were the priest and the Levite merely callous? Probably they thought the man dead and that, by touching him, they would make themselves unfit to perform their ritual duties (Num. 19.11). But if so, they put the claims of the Law before those of humanity.

When St Matthew and St. Luke concluded their accounts of the great Sermon which summarized Jesus' design for life in the Kingdom, they did so with the story of The Two Builders. And so may we. In almost every respect—literary structure, dramatic quality and local colour—Matthew's version is to be preferred:

Every one then who hears these words of mine and does them will be like a wise man who built his house upon the rock; and the rain fell, and the floods came, and the winds blew and beat upon that house, but it did not fall, because it had been founded on the rock.

And every one who hears these words of mine and does not do them will be like a foolish man who built his house upon the sand; and the rain fell, and the floods came, and the winds blew and beat against that house, and it fell; and great was the fall of it (Matt. 7.24-27; Luke 6.47-49).

The meaning is plain. The rock-built house stands for hearing and doing Christ's words; the sand-built house for hearing them only. The storm of the parable might be the Last Judgment; more probably it is any severe testing-time in a disciple's life. In such a time the secret of security will be a life built on active obedience to Christ's teaching. Obey me, says the Lord, and you will weather the storm; neglect my words, and you court disaster.

'*My* words . . .' Scholars have discovered a rabbinical parable which says something like this one: A man whose knowing exceeds his doing is like a tree with many branches and few roots. The difference between the rabbi's parable and that of Jesus is this, that Jesus makes all depend upon the doing of his own words. '*My* words', he says. No prophet ever spoke like this. What a tremendous claim! The Carpenter of Nazareth stands before men, and tells them that he has laid down principles of action which they will neglect at their eternal peril. His design for life is the only one that will last.

6

THE CRISIS OF THE KINGDOM

IN THE last group of parables we become aware of the skies
darkening, the tension mounting, the climax approaching...
Jesus saw his ministry, which was the inauguration of the
Kingdom, moving inexorably to a supreme crisis in God's
dealings with his people. Other Divine 'visitations' Israel had
known before (notably the Exodus and the Exile); this was to
be the Visitation *par excellence*:

> Therefore also the Wisdom of God said, 'I will send them
> prophets and messengers, some of whom they will kill and perse-
> cute, that the blood of all the prophets, shed from the foundation
> of the world, may be required of this generation' (Luke 11.49 f.;
> Matt. 23.34 f., Q).

We may determine the rough pattern of this crisis (a developing situation rather than a single event) from the rest of his
teaching.[1] On the one hand, it would bring doom and disaster, at the hands of Rome, for the Jewish people and temple,
because they had not fulfilled God's high purpose for them.
On the other, if it would mean death for the Servant Messiah,
with suffering for his followers, beyond that death lay the
triumph of God's cause in his own representative person and
the rise of the New Israel. And when this crisis at last became
inescapable, Jesus wept over the city:

> If thou hadst known in this day, even thou, the things which
> belong unto peace! But now they are hid from thine eyes. For ...
> they shall not leave in thee one stone upon another, because thou
> knewest not the time of thy visitation (Luke 19.42 ff.).

It is against this background that many of the parables
become pregnant with meaning.

[1] See my *Work and Words of Jesus*, chapter 13.

75

I

Consider first the saying about Weather Signs addressed to the multitudes:

When you see a cloud rising in the west, you say at once, 'A shower is coming'; and so it happens. And when you see the south wind blowing, you say, 'There will be scorching heat'; and it happens. You hypocrites! You know how to interpret the appearance of earth and sky; but why do you not know how to interpret the present time? (Luke 12.54-56).

'You men of Israel', says Jesus, 'have merely to glance at the sky or note the wind's direction, and you can tell the weather. But God is visiting his people in blessing and judgment, and you can't see it.'

Their leaders were equally myopic. More than once Jesus accused the Scribes and Pharisees of spiritual blindness (cf. Matt. 23.16-24); and it is no wild conjecture that the parable of The Eye as the Body's Lamp condemned their cecity:

The eye is the lamp of the body. So if your eye is sound, your whole body will be full of light; but if your eye is not sound, your whole body will be full of darkness. If then the light in you is darkness, how great is the darkness! (Matt. 6.22 f.; Luke 11.34-36, Q).

In them, as Israel's leaders, one might have expected to find that vision without which a nation perishes. But 'there are none so blind as those who will not see'. The Scribes and Pharisees refused to see. It was the measure of their 'darkness' that, when the signs of this supreme Visitation were abroad in the land, they yet remained obdurately blind to them. It was a case, said Jesus, of 'the blind leading the blind' (Luke 6.39; Matt. 15.14), and the end must be disaster.

The frivolous irresponsibility of his generation Jesus further condemned in the parable of The Playing Children:

To what then shall I compare the men of this generation, and what are they like? They are like children sitting in the market place and calling to one another,

'We have played the flute to you, and you have not danced;[1]
We have sung the funeral dirge to you, and you have not
wept!'

(Luke 7.31 f.; Matt. 11.16 f., Q).

His contemporaries reminded Jesus of the children he had
seen playing weddings and funerals in the market place, the
boys quarrelling with the girls, the girls with the boys. Nothing
would please them. Some had no relish for John's preaching of
repentance and called him a crazy ascetic. Others disliked his
own Good News and called him a *bon vivant* who loved sinners' company. And while they quarrelled, momentous things
were happening.

The parable of The Rich Fool has usually been taken as 'an
awful warning' against greed. But is it not more likely to have
been a parable of 'the times'?

The land of a rich man brought forth plentifully; and he
thought to himself, 'What shall I do, for I have nowhere to store
my crops?' And he said, 'I will do this: I will pull down my barns,
and build larger ones; and there I will store all my grain and my
goods. And I will say to my soul, Soul, you have ample goods
laid up for many years; take your ease, eat, drink, be merry!'
But God said to him, 'Fool! This night your soul is required of
you; and the things you have prepared, whose will they be?' (Luke
12.16-20).[2]

The introductory dialogue (Luke 12.13-15), with its invitation to Jesus to decide a family dispute over money, may well
preserve the original occasion. Refusing to arbitrate, Jesus told
them a story about a rich farmer, selfishly absorbed in money-
making and dreaming of a gay old age, when suddenly, in a
single night, his security was shattered. The man's decisive
confrontation by God in the midst of his money-making is the
climax of the story. May we not then read it as our Lord's
dramatic warning to the brothers—and all like them—to wake

[1] It was the boys who played at weddings (the round dance at a
wedding being the men's dance), the girls who preferred funerals.
Jeremias, op. cit., 161.
[2] On Luke 12.21, a generalizing conclusion, see Appendix 4. Since
D a b omit the verse, its authenticity is doubtful.

up to what is happening? 'You senseless creatures! Here you are squabbling about money—and catastrophe may overwhelm you any day!'

II

In the next four parables Jesus says to Israel's leaders, 'You have been unfaithful, and are in peril of judgment.'

The parable of The Savourless Salt has come down in three different versions. St Mark's is the shortest and simplest (Mark 9.50). St Matthew's, with its opening, 'You are the salt of the earth', is the correct interpretation for Christians (Matt. 5.13). But St Luke's may well be closest to what Jesus actually said:

> Salt is a good thing. But if salt becomes insipid, what will bring back its flavour? It is fit neither for the land nor the dunghill. So it is thrown out[1] (Luke 14.34 f.).

This is clearly a warning—a warning to Judaism. Supreme in their knowledge of God, the Jews should have been 'a savour of life' to the world. But they had lost their 'tang'— that saving knowledge of God which made them unique among the nations—and were in danger of being thrown on the scrap heap.

Of similar import is The Lamp and the Bushel, also found in Matthew, Mark and Luke. Here is St Matthew's version:

> Men do not light a lamp and put it under a meal-tub but on a stand, and it gives light to all in the house (Matt. 5.15; Luke 11.33; Mark 4.21).[2]

When darkness falls (says Jesus) and the lamp is lit, you don't proceed to put it below the meal-tub, do you? No, its proper place is the lamp-stand where its beam will benefit everybody. Yet this is what the Scribes and Pharisees have done with the light that was to 'lighten the Gentiles'.[3] En-

---

[1] My translation. 'Land' may be a mistranslation of an Aramaic word which meant 'seasoning'. In that case the translation would be: 'fit neither for seasoning nor for dunging.'

[2] Luke 11.33 reads, 'that those who come in may see the light', suggesting a reference to the Gentiles.

[3] The rabbis compared the *Torah* to a lamp. Cf. Ps. 119.105.

trusted with a revelation meant for all God's family, they have nevertheless, by their policy of selfish exclusiveness, hidden that revelation away and so thwarted God's purposes.

Here too belongs the parable of The Servant set in Authority:

Who then is the faithful and wise steward, whom his master will set over his household, to give them their portion of food at the proper time? Blessed is that servant whom his master when he comes finds so doing. Truly I tell you, he will set him over all his possessions. But if that servant says in his heart, 'My master is delayed in coming,' and begins to beat the men-servants and the maid-servants, and to eat and drink and get drunk, the master of that servant will come on a day when he does not expect him, and at an hour he does not know, and will punish him, and put him with the unfaithful (Luke 12.42-46; Matt. 24.45-51, Q).

The parable is a study in fidelity. As we have it now—see its context in Matthew—it is a warning to the Church's leaders to be faithful in the interval before Christ comes in glory. This was a natural re-application. But when Christ uttered it, the servant set in authority represented Israel's leaders, especially the Scribes. It was they whose fidelity was *sub judice*—and the *judex* God himself. Guardians of a Divine revelation, they had smothered it beneath a mass of pettifogging rules and regulations until the resultant load[1] of legalism might seem designed to drive men away from the Kingdom rather than bring them in (Luke 11.52; Matt. 23.13). And in the parable Jesus warns them that the day of God's reckoning is near when it will be revealed whether they have been faithful or not to their trust.[2]

A like warning is heard in The Talents (Matt. 25.14-30), with its Lukan counterpart, The Pounds (Luke 19.12-27). But Matthew's version is to be preferred, because Luke's has been conflated with another parable about a nobleman who went

[1] When Jesus said, 'Come unto me all you who are heavy laden' (Matt. 11.28), he was thinking of this load.
[2] Luke 12.47-48a, missing in Matthew, is a secondary expansion of the parable (Jeremias).

abroad to seek a kingdom—'the parable of the Prince Royal.'[1]

A man going on a journey called his servants and entrusted to them his property; to one he gave five talents, to another two, and to another one, to each according to his ability. Then he went away. He who had received the five talents went at once and traded with them; and he made five talents more. So too, he who had the two talents made two talents more. But he who had received the one talent, went and dug in the ground and hid his master's money.

Now after a long time the master of those servants came and settled accounts with them. And he who had received the five talents came forward, bringing five talents more, saying, 'Master, you delivered to me five talents; here I have made five talents more.' His master said to him, 'Well done, good and faithful servant; you have been faithful over a little, I will set you over much; enter into the joy of your master.' And he also who had the two talents came forward, saying, 'Master, you delivered to me two talents; here I have made two talents more.' His master said to him, 'Well done, good and faithful servant; you have been faithful over a little; I will set you over much; enter into the joy of your master.'

He also who had received the one talent came forward, saying, 'Master, I knew you to be a hard man, reaping where you did not sow, and gathering where you did not winnow; so I was afraid, and went and hid your talent in the ground. Here you have what is yours.' But his master answered him, 'You wicked and slothful servant! You knew that I reap where I have not sowed, and gather where I have not winnowed? Then you ought to have invested my money with the bankers, and at my coming I should have received what was my own with interest. So take the talent from him, and give it to him who has the ten talents' (Matt. 25.14-28).[2]

The story is about a man who, when he went from home, en-

---

[1] See Luke 19.12, 14, 15, 27. 'A nobleman went into a far country to receive kingly power and then return. But his citizens hated him and sent an embassy after him, saying, "We do not want this man to reign over us." When he returned, having received the kingly power, he said, "As for these enemies of mine, bring them here and slay them before me." '

This reads like the true story of Herod the Great's son Archelaus and the Jews of Judea, as told by Josephus. Excise these 'intrusions', and Luke's parable is basically the same as Matthew's.

[2] Matt. 25.29 f. probably did not originally belong to the parable. Verse 29 is a floating logion found elsewhere. Verse 30 has a 'Matthean' sound.

trusted his wealth to three servants, bidding them employ it well in his absence. On the master's return, two of the servants who had put their monies to good use were rewarded. The third who had done nothing with his was punished.

We may be sure Jesus was not moralizing generally about the right use of personal gifts, as preachers do today. The contexts show that both Matthew and Luke, by their placing of the parable, made it carry a lesson for the Church in the interval before Christ's Second Coming. Again, the re-application is fair enough. But if, ignoring it, we seek the original setting in the ministry of Jesus, two questions arise: Where does the stress fall in the story? And about whom did Jesus tell it?

In parables with three characters like this one, the spotlight falls, by the rule of 'end stress', on the third character in the story—that is, on the servant who did nothing with his money. Whom did this 'barren rascal' signify in the mind of Jesus? (The successful two, be it noted, are only there as foils to him.) Who was this 'slothful and wicked servant' whose caution amounted to a breach of trust? The answer is that he typified the pious Pharisee who hoarded the light God gave him (the Law) and kept for himself what was meant for mankind. Such a policy of selfish exclusivism yields God no interest on his capital; it is tantamount to defrauding him and must incur his judgment.[1] And the time for settling accounts is approaching.

III

The parables we have just been considering belong to the later phases of the ministry. So too, even more obviously, must the next group in which Jesus says: 'Unless you repent, God's judgment must fall.'

[1] From Ezra's time (444 BC) the Jews had sought to preserve their religion from heathen influence, and under the Pharisees an extreme nationalism had developed which embittered other nations against Israel. Their very zeal for the purity of their religion had sterilized it. They wanted to keep God for themselves alone.

The first is The Barren Fig Tree. It reminds us of Mark's Cursing of the Fig Tree which occurred at Bethany, after the Triumphal Entry.

> A man had a fig tree planted in his vineyard; and he came seeking fruit on it and found none. And he said to the vinedresser, 'Lo, these three years I have come seeking fruit on this fig tree, and I find none. Cut it down; why should it use up the ground?' And he answered him, 'Let it alone, sir, this year also, till I dig about it and put on manure. And if it bears fruit next year, well and good; but if not, you can cut it down' (Luke 13.6-9).

The fig tree certainly symbolizes Israel, sterile and unfruitful. A Jülicher-esque exegesis would dissuade us from identifying the man who came in search of fruit. But when we remember Mark 11.13 ('He went to see if he could find anything on it'), it is hard not to believe that by the man Jesus meant himself. The clear implication of the parable is that Israel's time for repentance is short; yet there remains a last chance—a reminder that God is merciful as well as just.

In the next parable, commonly called The Defendant, Jesus urges his hearers to seize that chance:

> As you go with your accuser before the magistrate, make an effort to settle with him on the way, lest he drag you to the judge, and the judge hand you over to the officer, and the officer put you in prison. I tell you, you will never get out till you have paid the very last copper (Luke 12.57-59; Matt. 5.25-26, Q).

Set in the Sermon on the Mount, these words read like a plain advice to the Christian to compose his quarrel with his opponent before it gets to actual litigation. But St Luke, who put the parable in a crisis context, evidently had an inkling of its original thrust. It is in fact a crisis parable. No man in his senses (it says) who knew he was bound to lose, would allow himself to see the inside of a law court. Long before it came in sight, he would settle with his opponent on the road. 'And you', says Jesus in effect to his hearers, 'are even now on your way to a much greater court. Come to God in penitence while you still have time.'

Here perhaps we may best take the parable of Dives and

Lazarus, which was probably addressed not to the Scribes and Pharisees but to the Sadducees[1] and forms Jesus' answer to their demand for a sign. (Mark 12.18-23 is evidence that Jesus at this time engaged in controversy with the Sadducees.)

There was a rich man, who was clothed in purple and fine linen and who feasted sumptuously every day. And at his gate lay a poor man named Lazarus, full of sores, who desired to be fed with what fell from the rich man's table; moreover, the dogs came and licked his sores. The poor man died and was carried by the angels to Abraham's bosom. The rich man also died and was buried; and in Hades, being in torment, he lifted up his eyes, and saw Abraham afar off and Lazarus in his bosom. And he called out, 'Father Abraham, have mercy upon me, and send Lazarus to dip the end of his finger in water and cool my tongue; for I am in anguish in this flame.' But Abraham said, 'Son, remember that you in your lifetime received your good things, and Lazarus in like manner evil things; but now he is comforted here and you are in anguish. And besides all this, between us and you a great chasm has been fixed, in order that those who would pass from here to you may not be able, and none may cross from there to us.' And he said, 'Then I beg you, father, to send him to my father's house, for I have five brothers, that he may warn them, lest they also come into this place of torment.' But Abraham said, 'They have Moses and the prophets; let them hear them.' And he said, 'No, father Abraham, but if some one goes to them from the dead, they will repent.' He said to him, 'If they do not hear Moses and the prophets, neither will they be convinced if some one should rise from the dead' (Luke 16.19-31).

The parable was probably based on a popular tale[2] about a rich man and a poor man and the reversal of their fortunes in the next life. It falls into two parts: (a) the story proper (19-26) with its account of what befell Dives and Lazarus when they died; and (b) the epilogue (27-31) where the demand for a sign is refused.

What sort of sign was demanded? It sounds as if the sceptical Sadducees had sought to evade Jesus' challenge by saying they might change their minds about the future life if only he would give them some spectacular sign in proof of it. Jesus

[1] T. W. Manson, The Sayings of Jesus, 296 f.
[2] So Gressmann and others.

uses this demand for a sign, which he refuses, in order to condemn their heartless selfishness.

In Part I his concern is not to give information about 'the temperature of Hell or the furniture of Heaven'; but he does insist that there *is* a future life and that the Sadducees' inhumanity has to do with their denial of it. The link between Part I and Part II is this: if inhumanity has such terrible consequences for men in the next world, surely some impressive sign should be given to warn them. If Dives (who symbolizes the Sadducees) had known what a 'roasting' was in store for him, how differently he would have treated Lazarus on earth! In the Epilogue this objection, spoken by Dives, is repelled. If a man (says Jesus) cannot be humane with the Old Testament in his hand and Lazarus on his doorstep, nothing—neither a visitant from the other world nor a revelation of the horrors of Hell—will teach him otherwise. Such requests for signs are pure evasions.

IV

The burden of the last group of parables—The Waiting Servants, The Burglar and The Ten Virgins—is: 'Be prepared!'

The first is that beautifully paraphrased in Philip Doddridge's hymn, 'Ye servants of the Lord.' Here are Luke's words:

Let your loins be girded and your lamps burning, and be like men who are waiting for their master to come home from the marriage feast, so that they may open to him at once when he comes and knocks. Blessed are those servants whom the master finds awake when he comes; truly I say to you, he will gird himself and have them sit at table, and he will come and serve them. If he comes in the second watch, or in the third, and finds them so, blessed are those servants! (Luke 12.35-38).

Like Doddridge, the early Christians took the parable as a summons to the Church to be alert for the Lord's Second Advent; and it is not hard to see how they adapted it for this purpose. (For example Luke 12.37b, which recalls John 13.4 f., is an allegorizing intrusion describing what Jesus had done and would do upon his Return.) But if you remove these additions[1] you are left with the picture of a great household 'tensed up' while the master, who may come back at any time, is away. Preparedness is the central idea.

Preparedness for the *Parousia*? So the early Church took it. But did Jesus? The crisis he had in mind was surely not that of a *Parousia* lying on the far side of his death, resurrection and ascension but the much more immediate one we have called 'the crisis of the Kingdom'. He may have been addressing the disciples (cf. Mark 14.38), or he may have been addressing the multitudes. In any case, he was trying to alert them for each stage of the developing crisis.

A like readiness is being enjoined in the little parable of The Burglar (Matt. 24.43; Luke 12.39,Q) which, in Luke, follows The Waiting Servants:

But know this, that if the householder had known at what hour the thief was coming, he would have been awake and would not have left his house to be broken into (Luke 12.39).

It reads like the ending of a vivid little tale from real life. No doubt there had been a recent burglary of which everybody was talking. 'Take a warning from your neighbour's experience', says Jesus, 'or you too may be caught unawares.' Once again Jesus is thinking of the time of stress inaugurated by the climax of his ministry—a time which would supervene upon them as suddenly as the Flood upon the antediluvians (Luke 17.26 f.)— and is seeking to put them in readiness for it. Later, when the Lord's return from heaven seemed to be delayed, the Church used the parable to inculcate vigilance (cf. I Thess. 5.2).

This is to be seen perhaps most clearly in the last parable of the group, The Ten Virgins:[2]

[1] See Dodd (op. cit., 160-167) and Jeremias (op. cit., 53-55), who point out that Mark's little parable of The Watchman (Mark 13.34-37) is a variant version of The Waiting Servants.
[2] Village girls, perhaps neighbours' children—not bridesmaids. For bridesmaids (a) would not have been on the road, but with the bride; (b) would not have been expected to supply their own oil; and (c) would not have been excluded from the wedding ceremony.

Then the kingdom of heaven shall be compared to ten maidens who took their lamps and went to meet the bridegroom. Five of them were foolish, and five were wise. For when the foolish took their lamps, they took no oil with them; but the wise took flasks of oil with their lamps. As the bridegroom was delayed, they all slumbered and slept. But at midnight there was a cry, 'Behold the bridegroom! Come out to meet him.' Then all those maidens rose and trimmed their lamps. And the foolish said to the wise, 'Give us some of your oil, for our lamps are going out.' But the wise replied, 'Perhaps there will not be enough for us and for you; go rather to the dealers and buy for yourselves.' And while they went to buy, the bridegroom came, and those who were ready went in with him to the marriage feast; and the door was shut. Afterwards the other maidens came also, saying, 'Lord, Lord, open to us.' But he replied, 'Truly, I say to you, I do not know you.' Watch therefore, for you do not know the day or the hour (Matt. 25.1-13).

The parable, as it now stands in Matthew, refers to the Second Advent. This is shown by the 'then' of verse 1, and by the command 'Watch therefore' of the last verse. But the 'then' is Matthew's, and the command must have been added by the early Church, since manifestly it does not fit the parable—all the maidens, wise as well as foolish, 'slumbered and slept'!

What has happened is clear. The Church, noting the words 'As the bridegroom delayed' (verse 5), has turned what was originally a story about an earthly wedding into an allegory of Christ the heavenly Bridegroom, thus making the parable a summons to Christians to be ready for the Second Advent.[1]

We need not be scornful of the early Church's procedure, for all of us who preach the parables today re-apply them to our own situation 'between the times', whether we allegorize them or not. But in our Lord's mouth the parable was a realistic story[2] about a village wedding at which some of the guests turned up late; and he used it to alert the Jewish people to the impending crisis set in motion by his ministry. 'And the door was shut', we read. 'The door that has been closed', said the Jewish proverb, 'is not quickly opened.' So, in his parable,

[1] The scribe who added the words 'and the bride' in verse 1 (found in Codex Bezae and some other MSS.) evidently had the same idea.
[2] Cf. the Jewish proverb: 'The six-year-old and the sixty-year-old will run after the sound of the marriage drum.'

Jesus said to his hearers: 'The crisis is at hand, and will bring with it inexorable severance. Be prepared for it!'

One great parable which has many allegorical features preserves Jesus' final warning to the Sanhedrin (Mark 11.27; 12.12). It is the parable of The Wicked Vinedressers, which might well be renamed the parable of The Owner's Son:

A man planted a vineyard, and set a hedge around it, and dug a pit for the winepress, and built a tower, and let it out to tenants, and went into another country. When the time came, he sent a servant to the tenants, to get from them some of the fruit of the vineyard. And they took him and beat him, and sent him away empty-handed. Again he sent to them another servant, and they wounded him in the head, and treated him shamefully. And he sent another, and him they killed; and so with many others, some they beat and some they killed. He had still one other, a beloved son; finally he sent him to them, saying, 'They will respect my son.' But those tenants said to one another, 'This is the heir; come, let us kill him, and the inheritance will be ours.' And they took him and killed him, and cast him out of the vineyard. What will the owner of the vineyard do? He will come and destroy the tenants, and give the vineyard to others (Mark 12.1-9).

In spite of scholarly doubts, there is no cogent reason for questioning its substantial authenticity.[1] In its complete silence about the Resurrection, it is quite unlike the kind of thing some later Christian might have invented. The prophetic passage about God's climactic visitation of his people, which we quoted at the beginning of this chapter, is solid evidence that Jesus did say things like this. And, in short, it is altogether probable that Jesus did, during his last week in Jerusalem, use all the resources of his imagination to bring home to the Sanhedrin their awful responsibility before God in rejecting his Messiah.

In the agrarian discontent of the time, the parable might well have been an actual story of what happened to an absentee landlord's property. But it was not—and the Jewish leaders knew it (Mark 12.12)! The parable is our Lord's picture of Israel's story through the long centuries. Thus and thus did God in his grace deal with his people; and thus and thus did

[1] See Appendix 3.

they deal with the messengers he sent them: 'O Jerusalem, Jerusalem that killest the prophets and stonest them that are sent unto thee . . .' And now matters are mounting to their awful climax . . . In a sense, the tale was autobiography; the Man who told it was its central figure; and within a few days of his telling it, it came true. God sent his 'only son' to Israel, making his last appeal; and they slew him, on an April morning, outside the northern wall of Jerusalem.

No full length parable survives to tell how the Messiah conceived the purpose of his dying; but the Gospel tradition preserves three miniature parables which take us some way into the secret: the sayings about the Cup, the Baptism and the Ransom. He was drinking 'the cup our sins had mingled' (Mark 10.38; 14.36). He was undergoing a baptism of blood whereby others might be cleansed (Luke 12.50; Mark 10.38). As the Servant Messiah, he was giving his life to 'ransom the many' (Mark 10.45).

One parable—if we may call it so, for it is part similitude, part allegory, part apocalyptic—we have not mentioned, that of The Sheep and the Goats: [1]

> When the Son of man comes in his glory,
>   And all the angels with him,
> Then he will sit on his glorious throne.
>   Before him will be gathered all the nations
>   And he will separate them one from another
>   As a shepherd separates the sheep from the goats,
>   And he will place the sheep at his right hand, but the goats at
>   the left.
>
> Then the King will say to those at his right hand,
>   'Come, O blessed of my Father,
>   Inherit the kingdom prepared for you from the foundation of
>   the world;

For I was hungry	and you gave me food:
I was thirsty	and you gave me drink:
I was a stranger	and you welcomed me:
I was naked	and you clothed me:
I was sick	and you visited me:
I was in prison	and you came to me.'

[1] We follow Théo Preiss's arrangement, which clearly brings out its poetical structure. See *Life in Christ*, 44 f.

Then the righteous will answer him,
'Lord,
  When did we see thee hungry and feed thee?
    or thirsty and give thee drink?
  When did we see thee a stranger and welcome thee?
    or naked and clothe thee?
  When did we see thee sick or in prison and visit thee?'

And the King will answer them,
  'Truly I say to you, As you ministered[1] to one of the least of
  these my brethren, you ministered to me.'

Then he will say to those at his left hand,
  'Depart from me, you cursed, into the eternal fire prepared
    for the devil and his angels;
  for I was hungry   and you gave me no food:
    I was thirsty   and you gave me no drink:
    I was a stranger and you did not welcome me:
    naked   and you did not clothe me:
    sick and in prison and you did not visit me.'

Then they also will answer,
  'Lord, when did we see thee hungry,
    or thirsty,
    or a stranger,
    or naked,
    or sick,
    or in prison
  and did not minister to thee?'

Then he will answer them,
  'Truly I say to you, As you ministered not to one of the least
  of these, you ministered not to me.'
  And they will go away into eternal punishment:
    But the righteous into eternal life

                               (Matt. 25.31-46).

This passage is one of the supreme glories of the New Testament, and, despite signs of stylization by the evangelist, con-

---

[1] Preiss, op. cit., 45 f., convincingly suggests that Jesus used the
Aramaic verb *abad*, which means both 'do' and 'serve'. This is con-
firmed by the fact that in their reply the condemned use the verb
'serve' (*diakoneo*), which breaks the symmetry otherwise so strict in
Greek but presumably did not break it in the original Aramaic.

tains too many originalities not to go back to Jesus himself.[1]

How shall we interpret it? Much turns on how we take the phrase 'the least of these my brethren'[2] (verse 40). Are they Christ's disciples? Or does the phrase describe all needy folk? We follow several modern scholars in taking the latter view. The parable may then be regarded as Christ's answer to the question: By what criterion will those who have not known Christ be judged on Judgment Day? The answer is: by the deeds of mercy they have shown to the needy and the outcast. In the persons of the poor and destitute men are confronted by the hidden Messiah, and to show love and pity to such is to show love to him. If heathen men have shown such love, they will have a share in the heavenly Kingdom.

Few passages so disclose the mind of Christ as this one does. None teaches more clearly that he who holds in his hands the destiny of all men cares so much about the last, the least and the lost. This is the Messiah whom we worship.

Our task of trying to restore the parables to their original settings is done, and unless we have completely failed, the truth of the new approach must be plain.

The parables are 'the precipitate of a campaign, the final step of which was Jesus' surrender to the Cross'.[3] First they illuminate the Good News with which Jesus began his ministry, telling how the Kingdom of God comes and grows. Next, they speak to us of the sovereign grace of the Father who brings the Kingdom. Third, they suggest some of the qualities that Jesus looked for in the men of the Kingdom. And, last of all, they take us some way into the meaning of that supreme crisis in which he who embodied in his own person God's saving sovereignty, went to his death, believing that by it the New Covenant would be established and the Kingdom 'opened to all believers'.

What happened is history. The day of reckoning came and

---

[1] See Appendix 3.
[2] The words 'my brethren' are omitted by B and some Old Latin Versions. They may have been a gloss.
[3] C. W. F. Smith, op. cit., 272.

the judgment of God, against which Jesus had warned them, fell upon the Jewish temple and people. But if the Old Israel fell from grace, the New Israel was born. By Christ's death and resurrection, the Kingdom of God 'came with power' (Mark 9.1; Rom. 1.4), the Holy Spirit descended on Jesus' waiting followers, and the new people of God, which is the Church of Christ, went forth from the Upper Room, 'conquering and to conquer'.

7

PREACHING THE PARABLES

How does all this new light on the parables affect those of us who have to find in them a Word of God for today?

One thing is uncomfortably clear. Much of what the scholars are telling us runs counter to interpretations of the parables long beloved of preachers and current in the Church. The awful question may be posing itself in some minds: must we, in honesty, forthwith consign the bulk of our old sermons on the parables to the waste-paper basket? Well, I cannot counsel such radical demolition. I would rather say that, if you are planning a homiletic holocaust, you should save from the flames all such sermons which have an authentic spiritual value of their own. For a true Word of the Lord may be drawn from a parable of Jesus even though it depends on a turn of meaning not uppermost in our Lord's mind when he spoke the parable.

I remember, for example, a fine sermon of George H. Morrison's on 'The Two Petitions of the Prodigal':

1. Father, give.
2. Father, make me.

and the theme was the contrast between the two attitudes of the Prodigal. To begin with, he knew no will but his own. But when 'he came to himself', his only desire was to obey his father's will. And, wonderful to tell, it was when he asked for nothing, that he got the very best. From these two texts Morrison drew a deeply Christian sermon on the difference which the coming of grace into a man's life ought to make.

I remember, again, a sermon of Kierkegaard's about penitence based on The Pharisee and the Publican. True penitence, (he says) means:

First: 'Being alone with God', as the Publican was. When we are alone with God, we realize how far from God we are.

Second: it means 'Looking downwards', as the Publican did; for when we see the majesty and holiness of God, we begin to realize our own littleness and weakness.

Third: it means 'Awareness of being in danger', as the Publican was aware when he cried, 'God be merciful to me a sinner'; for it is when we feel quite safe, like the Pharisee, we really are in peril.

Neither of these sermons directly reproduces the original thrust of the parable; but each puts across a piece of authentic Christian truth. Is not this the decisive test of a true sermon? The point to watch is that when we use the parables in the pulpit thus, we must be quite sure that what we say really represents Christ's mind as we have it in his recorded teaching. Here, as G. H. Boobyer puts it, 'Biblical scholarship rightly exercises an important function; for the spirit of the prophets should be subject not only to the prophets but also, to some extent, to the professors.'[1]

This said, let us consider what effect the modern study of the parables should have on our preaching. Down the centuries three main approaches to the parables have been proposed, and we may take them in turn.

I

The first is of course the *allegorizing* approach. Knowing what we now do about the parables, we may agree on this first principle: 'No more arbitrary allegorizing of the parables.'

By 'arbitrary' we mean 'Origenesque'. Origen and Augustine were great princes of the Church from whom we may still learn much—but *not* about the interpretation of the parables. To persist, at this time of day, in that kind of exegesis is to sin against the fuller light which God has given us through his servants, the great Christian scholars of our time.

We know that Christ never meant the Good Samaritan to

[1] *The Expository Times*, Feb., 1951.

be a cryptograph for himself, or the Inn for the Church, or the 'two pence' for the two sacraments. We know that in The Sower the various percentages of the abundant harvest—30, 60 and 100%—do not signify the mass of Christians, the Gospel celibates and the martyrs. We know that in The Leaven the 'three measures of meal' represent a normal baking amount and not the three parts of man—body, soul and spirit—or the three known parts of the world. We know that the 'oil' in the story of the Ten Virgins is simply a bit of the dramatic machinery of the parable—or, rather, something that helps its wheels to turn—and not faith, or charity, or alms-giving, or good works, or the Holy Spirit, or joy, or what have you. In short, this sort of allegorical *eisegesis* (for it is not *exegesis*) is, as the Germans say, *streng verboten*.

But is allegorizing in every shape and form excluded from a true interpretation of the parables? Certainly not. We are agreed that our Lord's parables are, for the most part, similitudes, not allegories. But we are also agreed, I think, that some of these similitudes have allegorical elements, and that one indeed is an allegory: The Wicked Vinedressers. How shall we treat this allegorical parable? Shall we, with some scholars (e.g. F. C. Grant in *The Interpreter's Bible*), call it an early Christian invention because, among other things, it contains strong allegorical features? No, there are sound reasons for regarding it as substantially authentic. But there is another way of treating it which, in my view, is equally arbitrary, the way of Jeremias who has taught us so much. So strongly is he under the spell of Jülicher's 'one-point-per-parable' theory that this is what he says about it:

In the situation of Jesus, from whom alone the parable could have come, the allegorical application of 'the son' to the Son of God would have been entirely foreign to the minds of his audience.[1]

What then is the meaning of the parable? Jeremias answers: 'Like so many other parables of Jesus, it vindicates the offer

[1] Op. cit., *first edition*, p. 57. This statement is modified in the revised edition (p. 72).

of the Gospel to the poor.'[1] This, I confess, seems to me a choice example of how doctrinaire theory can lead a fine exegete astray. Jeremias is forcing the parable into a mould which cannot hold it, in the interests of a one-point theory applied with too much vigour and rigour.

This parable aside, how far ought we to admit allegorical interpretations into our exegesis?

The history of their interpretation has warned us not to make too rigorous a distinction between parable and allegory. As we have seen, the Old Testament *mashal* describes figurative sayings of many kinds; and in the Old Testament we find not only pure similitudes and story parables but also allegories. Furthermore, we have seen that rabbinical parables sometimes contained definite allegorical features. *A priori*, then, we have no right to say that Jesus' parables must have been completely innocent of allegory. In fact, they were not.

Are there any rules we can lay down for interpreters about where allegorizing should begin and end? Some of the wisest things ever said on this score were said by James Denney in *The Expositor* for August and September, 1911. After declaring that no aesthetic scruples would have prevented Jesus using allegory if it had suited his purpose and that the interpreter of the parables should use his trained judgment on the matter—like a sensible man and not like a pedant—he answered our question something like this (I summarize for brevity's sake): 'The golden rule is this: Don't try in the interests of an arbitrary theory to eliminate everything allegorical and so trim the texts into pure parables. On the other hand, don't allegorize to the point which mars the one lesson which every parable was meant to teach.'

I call this wise counsel, and I would like to suggest a touchstone for detecting genuine allegorical elements in the parables.

Jesus, let us remember, intended his parables to be meaningful to his hearers. If then you meet something in a parable which almost cries out to be taken symbolically, i.e. allegorically, stop and ask yourself: would this detail carry this sym-

[1] Op. cit., 76.

bolical significance for the men to whom Jesus spoke? If so, we may fairly take it so. In practice, what it amounts to is this. Elements in a parable which, either in the Old Testament or in current Jewish theology, bore a familiar symbolical meaning, and were therefore likely to be so taken by Jesus' audience, should be so interpreted. If The Wicked Vinedressers refers to a vineyard, especially against the background of Isa. 5 which it echoes, we are entitled to say: The vineyard is Israel. If in The Sower and other parables we find a reference to 'the harvest', we remember that the harvest was a familiar Jewish symbol for 'the day of the Lord', and interpret accordingly. If in The Mustard Seed we find a closing reference to 'the birds of the air' coming to roost in the tree's branches, we remember that in rabbinical circles 'the birds of the air' commonly signified the Gentiles, and we so interpret it in the parable.

The one thing to remember is that we must 'never allegorize to the point which mars the one lesson which every parable was meant to teach'.

II

Allegorizing of the Origen-esque sort is clearly out. On what lines, then, should we preachers approach our task of expounding the parables?

Except in places where the bad old allegorizing lingered on, the commonest approach during the last hundred years has been the *moralizing* one.

You remember how Jülicher did it. Having proscribed allegory, he proceeded to draw from each parable one simple moral which he declared was the lesson Jesus meant it to teach. No need to try to identify the various talents in the parable; for its message was simply: 'fidelity in all that God has entrusted to us', or alternatively: 'reward is only earned by performance'. Similarly, the moral of The Unjust Steward was: 'use the present wisely if you want to make sure of a happy future.' And so on. The Founder of the Faith was evidently the Moralizer *par excellence*.

It is easy to make fun of Jülicher; but before we grow too hilarious, let us look at our own sermons. Don't we in fact do very much the same? Nay, don't we sometimes out-Jülicher Jülicher? Not content with one moral, we find two or even three!

Nor is it only the ordinary preacher who moralizes the parables. Distinguished expositors apparently do the same. I turn to one who was known as 'a prince of exegetes', Marcus Dods, to see what he makes of The Leaven: [1]

This parable (he explains) describes how Christianity changes the world, and this theme he develops under two heads. First: the change Christianity works on the world is inward, not outward; that is, Christianity dislikes violent changes,[2] preferring to accept things as it finds them and to leaven all it touches. Second: it works its changes by the power of personal influence—by 'mixing' (as in the parable)—by the contact of Christians with non-Christians; and the secret of such influence is in having oneself a character which will communicate good.

The whole exposition is full of such unexceptional moralizing; but at the end, you have an uneasy feeling that the total effect is decidedly 'flattening' and a doubt whether this was just the point Jesus had in mind in his parable.

'It is not', Dods explains, 'the agency of God in the matter which Jesus wishes to illustrate here.' My own view would be that it is precisely this Divine agency which he is illustrating—the Rule of God (a dynamic thing) acting like a ferment in the world. But when I read such expositions of The Leaven, I am always reminded of a remark of James Denney's. Once, meeting John Hutton in Glasgow on his way to preach, Denney asked him what his sermon was to be. 'The parable of the Leaven.' 'And the line you are going to take?' 'Oh, the quiet leavening influence of Christianity.' 'Hutton', said Denney, 'Did you ever see a piece of leaven under a microscope?'

[1] *The Parables of our Lord*, Series I, 67-87.
[2] Cf. Luke 12.49-51: 'I came to cast fire upon the earth. . . . Do you think that I have come to give peace on earth? No, I tell you, but rather division.'

4

Let us take another instance. Dr George Buttrick is deservedly reckoned one of the greatest American preachers, as his volume on the parables is widely used. It is a fresh and vivid book; so I turned it up to see what Dr Buttrick had to say about The Labourers in the Vineyard:

'Though this parable does not prescribe industrial methods', he writes, 'we cannot read it, even casually, without seeing the fingers of Jesus probing beneath the surface of the vast realm of "business". Is a man out of work because he will not work? Jesus has no saving grace for such a man except the saving grace of adversity. Is a man out of work because of the callousness of a society which will not seriously grapple with the curse of unemployment? That tragedy smites Jesus to the core! He could never have told this story if he had not been moved with pity as he saw men idle in the market place. What would Jesus say, were he here in the flesh, to the corporation which dismisses men without the direst necessity; or to a labour union which "strikes" on a negligible pretext; or to business brains too absorbed with profits to address themselves to the poor man's problem of insecurity of occupation? This is not an economic tract but it is a demand that industry shall exist for man, and not man for industry.'[1]

On which the only comment is that it is nothing of the kind. By what stretch of the imagination can this be called legitimate exegesis of the parable? Does it not in fact miss the whole point of it, and make Jesus moralize about issues which have little or no connexion with the parable? 'We cannot', says Dr Buttrick, 'read the parable, even casually, without seeing the fingers of Jesus probing beneath the surface of the vast realm of "business".' I think we can. Indeed, it would need a reading the very reverse of casual to find such truths in this parable of Jesus. I too see 'probing fingers' in this exposition of the parable; but they are the fingers not of Jesus but of George A. Buttrick.

But, to be brief and candid about all this, don't we all go in for this kind of moralizing? Isn't it a commonplace of the

[1] *The Parables of Jesus*, 161.

preacher's technique? Isn't it something with a very long history behind it, something indeed which, as Jeremias has shown, goes back to the Evangelists themselves?

If St Matthew, for example, used the parables in this hortatory or moralizing way, are we entitled to do the same? Like St Matthew, we have sometimes to use for the edifying of the faithful what was originally spoken by Jesus in challenge to his critics. It is a case of adapting existing materials to meet changing needs; and the question is: how far ought we to yield to this pressure to moralize?

Recent work on the parables has made the question more urgent. So long as moralizing had the authoritative backing of scholars like Jülicher, we could engage in moralizing with a clear conscience believing that all Jesus' parables were originally meant to receive such treatment. But now that Dodd and Jeremias have shown us that many of Christ's parables took their origin in that great crisis of history which was the coming of the Kingdom of God and were designed to alert men to the gravity of that crisis, are we justified in continuing to preach them in the way that Dods and Buttrick did? Should we not rather put an embargo on all moralizing of the parables?

Well, if you wish my opinion, I think that total abstinence here would be a counsel of perfection, and that what we ought to aim at is rather temperance. For consider. Many of Christ's parables sketch a type of human conduct in vivid colours, and the hearers are expected to apply the story to their own lives either as an example or a warning. Good instances are The Two Builders, The Two Sons, The Pharisee and the Publican, and The Good Samaritan. These illustrate the parable as 'an ethical type' (T. W. Manson), and moralizing here is not only excusable but unavoidable. But even in the case of parables more directly related to the crisis, it cannot be wrong to moralize sometimes. After all, many of the crisis parables called for repentance, and a repentance which does not have clear and strong moral implications is not worthy of the name. No, what is to be avoided like the plague is *indiscriminate* moralizing. I am thinking of ministers who go to the parables for guidance on politics, economics, eugenics, pacifism, capital punishment, etc. This, in my judgment, we have no right to do. On the other hand, a temperate moralizing cannot be wrong, provided that we know what we are doing and ensure that our moralizing of the parables is, as Paul would say, *kata Christon*—that is, in accordance with the revealed mind of Christ.

But now, as the Apostle would say, 'I show you a more excellent way.'

III

Ideally, at any rate, all sound Christian preaching based on the parables ought to begin with the primary meaning of the parable—that is, the meaning it had when Jesus uttered it. The expositor's first task should be to discover what the Germans call the *Sitz im Leben Jesu* of the parable—its original setting in the ministry of Jesus. To whom did Jesus speak the parable? Why did he speak it? And, to use the old definition, what 'heavenly meaning' did he expect his hearers to take from the 'earthly story'? Our first concern should be the original 'thrust' of the parable. When we have found it, our next task is its translation into contemporary terms. Then, if we want to moralize, or warn, or instruct, or exhort, we shall be doing so on a dominical basis.

What this means in actual homiletic practice, we can best learn by taking a few examples.

Let us begin with The Sower, which is a parable of the Kingdom's coming. It presents us with a special problem because, as we saw, it admits of two different interpretations.

Most modern exegetes find the parable's main point in the abundant harvest. Thus Jeremias[1] says:

Jesus is full of joyful confidence; he knows that God has made a beginning, bringing with it a harvest of reward beyond all asking or conceiving. In spite of all failures, the Kingdom of God comes at last.

[1] Op. cit., 150.

On this view, the parable was originally a message of encouragement to faint-hearted disciples, and such it will remain when we preach it today. Now as then, Christ's servants, faced with the giant power of evil and observing how many foes are ranged against God's Kingdom in the world, may be tempted sometimes to doubt whether indeed the Lord God omnipotent reigneth. It is then, with Christ's warrant, that we must proclaim that his Kingdom 'stands and grows for ever', that we live in a world in which Jesus Christ has risen from the dead and now reigns in grace over his Church, that 'the little flock' he died to redeem now numbers seven hundred millions in the wide earth, and that the God who has already done so much to save us may be trusted to finish his work.

But it is also possible to read the parable as a parabolic comment on 'Take heed how you hear.' On this view, the parable shows how the same Word of God gets a different reception from different people. Addressed to the multitudes, it was originally a challenging word on the responsibility of hearing the Gospel of the Kingdom: a word gaining its urgency from the fact that he who preached it was the Messiah, that the Kingdom had come and was confronting men with the need for decision. And such the parable remains today, facing the hearer with the very pointed and personal question, 'What kind of soil am I?'

Have we then to choose between these two ways of treating the parable, or is there a third possibility? I think there is. Vincent Taylor,[1] who agrees that the main point lies in the abundant harvest, comments:

It is not necessary to regard the birds, the thorns and the rocky ground as simply the dramatic machinery of the story. These references reflect the experience of Jesus and his sense of the importance of attentive hearing.

'The importance of attentive hearing . . .' Does not this suggest that the most effective sermon would be one which used *both* interpretations? It would be, first, a ringing word

St Mark, 91.

of assurance to God's despondent servants in our day, and, second, a challenge to the right hearing of the Word.

I have already indicated how, on the first interpretation, we should make the parable relevant for today. But, on the second interpretation, it can be made equally contemporary.[1] For it is still Jesus, the Church's risen and regnant Lord who, through the ministry of the Word and Sacraments, sows the good seed in men's hearts. But the Word may be received today in such different ways: still, as in Christ's day, we have superficial hearers, or short-lived enthusiasts, or disciples torn by distracting interests, as well—thank God—as those who hear the Word and obey it.

From our second group of parables ('The Grace of the Kingdom') let us choose the Pharisee and the Publican, and consider how we should treat it in the pulpit.

On Jesus' lips it was addressed to those 'who trusted in themselves that they were righteous and despised others'. No need to doubt this statement of Luke's or question that Jesus was speaking to Pharisees. Neither is there any need to re-draw his vivid picture of the Pharisee 'standing by himself' and 'swanking' to God of his religious achievements—as though Omniscience did not know them—while the Publican, 'afar off' and with downcast eyes, confesses his own great unworthiness and throws himself on the mercy of God. The thing to notice is Jesus' verdict on the two men: 'God has justified the one, not the other.' 'Justified (accepted, forgiven) is one of Paul's favourite words. But if we suppose that 'justification by grace through faith' (to define it fully and accurately) is a doctrine peculiar to Paul, we are grievously mistaken. It is the Lord's also. When Christ declared that he came 'not to call the righteous but sinners' and (in the First Beatitude) that 'the beggars before God were blessed', he was proclaiming the same truth. The Pharisee and the Publican is that doctrine made into a parable, and it is in terms of the same saving truth that we ought to preach it today.

There is, of course, one big difference between Christ's

[1] C. E. B. Cranfield, *Scottish Journal of Theology*. Dec., 1951.

preaching of it and Paul's. When Paul says that acceptance with God comes to the sinner not through 'works' (like the Pharisee's) but through faith (like the Publican's), it is the faith of a man who, knowing his own sinfulness, lays hold on 'the finished work' of Christ and presents it to God saying, 'I believe that the Son of God loved me and gave himself for me' (Gal. 2.20): —

> For lo, between our sins and their reward
> We set the passion of thy Son, our Lord.

In Christ's teaching there is no such reference to the Cross. How could there be? Nevertheless, when we, who live on the Resurrection side of the Cross, preach justification by faith today, we are entitled to put the Cross into our preaching. To exclude it would be to reckon the Cross of no importance for our salvation, a thing incredible for any true Christian.

But do people need to hear the doctrine of this parable today? Certainly they do. It is a complete delusion to think that legalism is dead. Campbell Moody tells us: [1]

When I was a student, it seemed to me impossible that the errors of legalism, so thoroughly exposed by St Paul, could still survive. By and by I found, by conversation with men both in Christian and in heathen lands, how much I was mistaken. Everywhere men seek as of old to satisfy their conscience by the performance of duty, or by telling themselves that they have done their duty, or that at least they are as good as those who make a profession of their religion, and perhaps better, for they are not hypocrites.

Campbell Moody is right. Many people—church people no less than multitudes outside the Church who would not call themselves atheists—still try to square their consciences by telling themselves that they have done their duty, and for the rest, they put their faith in an easy-osy God like Omar Khayyám's:

> He's a Good Fellow and 'twill all be well.

Tell them that the Almighty God is gracious, speak to them

[1] *The Purpose of Jesus,* 141 f.

of his forgiveness, and they listen without understanding, persuaded that they have no need to repent. Only when they learn how insufficient is all their boasted goodness—only when they become dissatisfied not with this or that fault in their lives but with their whole character, that they are ready to cry with the Publican, 'God be merciful to me a sinner!' or with Thomas Chalmers, 'What could I do if God did not justify the ungodly?'—only then will they realize that the Gospel speaks to their condition and offers them the remedy they need. 'It is the beggars before God who are blessed', said the Lord. 'Yes', added Martin Luther, 'and we are all beggars.' But not till we know that we are beggars can we receive God's grace. This is the truth of our parable, and it is timeless.

From our third group of parables ('The Men of the Kingdom') let us choose The Unjust Steward—or, as we would call him in Scotland, 'the rascally factor'.

The story (let us recall) is of the estate-manager who, when he mismanaged his master's property and was dismissed, astutely saw that friendship was likely to be more use to him than hard cash. So, summoning two of his master's chief debtors, he invited them, with their own hands, to reduce the amounts of their indebtedness. 'How much do you owe my master?' 'A hundred quarters of wheat.' 'Very well, here is your bill . . . just enter eighty.' Thus, by sacrificing his own 'commission', the steward secured his future and a roof over his head. 'And the Lord', we read, 'praised the unjust steward because he had acted wisely; for the sons of this world are wiser in their generation than the sons of light.'

It is the steward's 'savvy' in a crisis—his 'rummel gumption', as Chalmers would have called it—that is applauded, and the applauder is Christ himself. If, as Luke says, Jesus was addressing his disciples, his meaning was something like this: 'Oh, if only my disciples would show as much practical prudence in God's affairs as the worldlings do in theirs!'

How shall we preach this parable? Leslie Weatherhead[1] has

[1] *In Quest of a Kingdom*, 233-243.

a sermon on the subject. He thinks that in the parable Christ is saying three things to Christians:

First: 'Learn from the shrewd, resourceful way in which the sons of this age do their business.'
Second: 'Invest in friendship.'
Third: 'Wrest triumph from disaster by creative living.'

Point 3, 'Wrest triumph from disaster by creative living', is the kind of point we should expect from one who is an eminent Christian psychologist. I have no doubt that it provides an excellent subject for a sermon. Not so long ago I heard just such a one in which the preacher began by telling us how the great ballerina, Alicia Markova, began her dancing career by doing remedial exercises for *flat feet*! Moreover, as he proceeded to say, the Bible has many examples of how men out of weakness became strong. We might even say that it often exhibits God himself wresting triumph from disaster. The stories of the Exodus, of the Exile and, above all, of the Cross leap to mind at once. And we might add that Christians are called to turn their tragedies into triumphs and to help other people to do the same.

But my criticism of Weatherhead is that such a theme does not lie along the line of the parable's central thrust. The steward's life, after he 'got the sack', could hardly be called a 'triumph'; and *expertise* on the account books is an odd recipe for 'creative living'.

Lesson 2 in Weatherhead, 'Invest in friendship', seems to depend on Luke 16.9: 'Make to yourselves friends of the mammon of unrighteousness': a saying which, according to most modern scholars, had no original connexion with it, though it immediately follows the parable.

But Weatherhead's first point contains the true lesson of the parable, as exegetes from Calvin to T. W. Manson agree; and if we are to preach it today, it is on this point that we should lay all the stress. 'Oh, if only my Christians would bring to God's business some of the resourcefulness that men of the world bring to theirs!' It is thus that Dr L. H. Mitton has treated it in a notable sermon.[1] And indeed such prudence is often as far to seek among Christians today as it was among Christ's original disciples. P. T. Forsyth has commented on the off-hand way in which a serious man will often make up his mind on the most grave concern of life. Such a man's religious views 'are of the most casual kind'. 'If it were a business matter he would go into it. If it were a scientific question, he would train his mind and then examine. But his religion he does not.' For many churchmen, he says, religion is only a refuge and a balm, because 'jaded with the pursuit of this world', they come to church on Sundays fit for no more than 'a warm bath or a sacred concert'. And he asks: why don't people give to the high business of eternity some of the same effort that they give to the grave business of time?[2]

We do not need to look far afield for examples of this. Business tycoons slave day and night to make their pile. Ardent Communists, though they have no hope of a Hereafter, devote all their time and talents to spreading their propaganda and 'collaring' key positions in the trade unions. And, speaking generally, men are at great pains to insure themselves against all the chances and changes of this fleeting world, while neglecting to put themselves in a state of preparedness for the next one. 'Oh, if only my Christians . . .' Can we not hear Christ still saying this to his people?

Finally, from the fourth group ('The Crisis of the Kingdom') let us choose the parable of The Talents (in Luke, The Pounds).

The time-honoured way of treating the Talents is to regard them as personal endowments which God has given each man, and which God expects him to use to the best advantage in the work of the Church or the service of his fellow-men. Normally a word of sympathy and encouragement is thrown in for the one-talent man.

All this is fair enough, and Christian. But does such exposition show an understanding of the original thrust of the

[1] The Expository Times, July 1953.
[2] Positive Preaching and the Modern Mind, 132, 146.

parable? The best modern exegesis finds in the parable a stern warning addressed to the religious leaders of Israel; and the spotlight falls, as we saw, on the third character in the story—the 'barren rascal' who buried his talent. This slothful servant symbolizes Israel's leaders. God had called Israel to be, in the phrase of Athanasius, 'the sacred school of the knowledge of God for all mankind'; but by their sloth, their selfish exclusiveness, and their faithlessness the trustees of this unique revelation had betrayed their trust. In the parable therefore Jesus solemnly warns them that the day of the Divine reckoning with them is at hand. And it was, as history shows.

How do we translate this into contemporary terms? The important thing is to realize that the application today must be in terms of the Church of Christ, which is the New Israel. We of the Church—especially those of us who are leaders and teachers in it—are faced with the same Divine demands. (Indeed, is not our responsibility still greater, since we are the recipients of God's full and final revelation of himself in his Son and share in the Pentecostal gifts of the Holy Spirit?) 'Trade till I come', is still the Lord's charge to us, and the parable faces us with the question: is the Church, in which he has set us as ministers, fulfilling its God-given commission to a world that shows signs of drifting into humanism and atheism for lack of the saving truth with which we have been entrusted? Or, preoccupied and absorbed in its own ecclesiastical concerns and disabled by denominational differences and disputes, is the Church in fact 'blocking' the witness which God's People ought to be making to a sin-sick and fear-ridden world?

This surely is the thrust of the parable for Churchmen in the twentieth century. But within this larger context (and this might well be the second point in the sermon we preach) the parable also warns the individual Christian. Each member of Christ's Body has, as St Paul says, his own gift and function given him by God for the upbuilding of the Church and the spread of the Gospel. Is he using it as he should? Is he, by his words and works, witnessing to men whose he is and whom he seeks to serve? Or is he by his sloth, timidity or faithlessness failing the God who made him and the Lord who died to redeem him? Here, illustration must end. I am no expert on homiletics, and you can easily improve on the examples I have given. But I am sure that the approach suggested is the right one for all of us who have a concern for Biblical truth and are not content to repeat the old mistakes.

Space has not allowed me to discuss how we ought to preach the greatest parable of all: The Prodigal Son. But two things may be said of it now. First, the parable is concerned with essentially the same truth as that of The Pharisee and the Publican. Only in The Prodigal Son Jesus looks at the matter more from the Divine angle, as the sweep of his canvas is vaster.

Second: In a true sense, the doctrine of this parable should form the burden and background of all our preaching. Somebody once asked John MacNeill, the celebrated Scottish evangelist, if he never preached from John 3.16. 'Na, na', said John, 'I have *that* in every sermon I preach.' Should we not be able to say much the same thing about the immortal story of the father and his two sons—the two lost sons?

Let me end on a general note. When I was a working minister, my understanding of the parables was very defective, so that I did not make nearly enough use of them in my preaching. I am now convinced that we ought to turn to them regularly for the material of our sermons, and that we ought to preach them in a vivid, modern and challenging way. Here, so far as technique is concerned, the great masters of preaching—from John Chrysostom and Luther to Phillips Brooks and James S. Stewart—can show us, by their practice, how to do it.

One practical suggestion I have to offer. No minister's 'barrel' is complete without a series of sermons on the chief parables. But when ought we to preach them? If one season of the year is more appropriate than another, it is the season of Lent. In the five Sundays of Lent when we should be remembering our Lord's ministry from the Temptation to the Cross, what finer spiritual teaching could there be for our people than our Lord's own commentary in parable on his ministry? We might start with The Sower or The Mustard Seed and end with The Wicked Vinedressers or The Last Judgment, and in between there are all the parables about the grace of God and the Christian life: enough indeed not for one Lent but for two or three Lents.

My main concern, however, is to drive you back to a study of the parables. As we have seen, they comprise more than one third of Jesus's recorded words, and they preserve, in Jeremias's phrase, 'a fragment of the original rock of the tradition'. In teaching our people the parables, we are putting them in direct contact with the declared mind of Christ. What better service could we do them?

> *Bewildered, dejected and prone to despair,*
> *To Thee as at first do we turn and beseech:*
> *Our ears are all open: give heed to our prayer;*
> *O Son of man, teach!*

THE PROBLEM OF MARK 4.11-13

(10) And when he was alone, those who were about him with the twelve asked him concerning the parables. (11) And he said to them, To you has been given the secret of the kingdom of God, but for those outside everything is in parables (12) so that they may indeed see but not perceive, and may indeed hear but not understand; lest they should turn again, and be forgiven. (13) And he said to them, Do you not understand this parable? How then will you understand all the parables?

The prima facie meaning of Mark 4.10 f. is that Jesus deliberately used parables to blind 'those outside' (the crowds as distinct from the disciples) and so make them ripe for rejection. This is simply absurd. Many solutions of the difficulty have been suggested. Here are three, all different, proposed by C. H. Dodd, T. W. Manson and J. Jeremias.

1. Dodd[1] (with many continental scholars) takes the disputed saying to be a later church construction, not a saying of Jesus. He translates:

To you is granted the mystery of the kingdom of God, but to those outside everything comes in parables, in order that they may look and look but never see, listen and listen but never understand, lest they should be converted and forgiven.

Finding here words reminiscent of St Paul's vocabulary, he thinks the saying reflects the doctrine of the early Church that the Jews were providentially blinded to the significance of Christ's coming. In other words, this explanation of the purpose of parables is an answer to a question which arose after Jesus' death and the failure of his followers to convert the Jewish people.

A simple solution but a drastic one.

2. T. W. Manson[2] considers the saying a genuine word of

[1] Op. cit., 13-15. [2] *The Teaching of Jesus*, 78-80.

Jesus but thinks that v.12 conceals a mistranslation from the Aramaic. He translates:

To you is given the secret of the kingdom of God; but all things come in parables to those outside who
> See indeed but do not know,
> And hear indeed but do not understand,
>> Lest they should repent and receive forgiveness.

The valuable point in Manson's discussion is his perception that v. 12, which quotes Isa. 6.9 f., reflects not the Hebrew or the LXX but the Targum.[1] (For example, the Targum ends, 'be forgiven', whereas the Heb. has, 'be healed' and the LXX, 'I will heal them'.) Now for most people the stumbling block in Mark's Greek is the *hina* ('that'). But the Targum here has the Aramaic word *de* which, besides meaning 'that', can also mean 'who'. Hence the right rendering of the passage would have been: '*Who* see indeed, etc.'

The parable, Manson says, is a test of a man's insight, and determines whether he will get into the Kingdom or stay outside it. Now, with this amended translation, the real cause of 'the outsiders'' blindness becomes their own fatal self-satisfaction. They do not wish to repent and be forgiven. (If they did, God would forgive them.) It is the hardness of the hearers' hearts which defeats the purpose of the parables.

On this view, Jesus does not quote the Isaiah passage to explain the purpose of the parables but to illustrate what is meant by 'those outside'. They are the people who lack the insight and faith which Jesus was constantly seeking.

This view seems to us more satisfactory than Dodd's.

3. Jeremias[2] accepts Manson's point about the Targum but does not believe that the saying originally referred to teaching by parables. He translates:

To you God has given the secret of the kingdom of God; but to those who are outside everything is obscure, in order that they (as it is written) 'may see and yet not see, may hear and yet not understand, unless they turn and God will forgive them'.

---

[1] The Aramaic paraphrase of an O.T. passage used in the synagogues.   [2] Op. cit., 13-19.

This is a genuine saying of Jesus but it deals not with parables but with Jesus' teaching in general. It is a sombre comment by the Lord on his mission (uttered perhaps after his unsuccessful ministry to the Galilean cities: Luke 10.13-15; Matt. 11.20-24,Q). 'The secret of the present kingdom is disclosed to the disciples, but to the outsiders the words of Jesus remain obscure because they do not recognize his mission or repent. Thus for them the terrible oracle of Isa. 6.10 is fulfilled. Yet a hope still remains: if they repent, God will forgive them.'

Here are the chief points in his discussion:

(a) Various features show v. 11 f. to be an insertion into an older context. Since this is so, we must, when interpreting, ignore its present context.

(b) The saying is early, Palestinian and probably authentic, since it agrees with the Targum and contains several Aramaisms.[1]

(c) We should translate v. 11: 'To you God has given the secret of the kingdom of God (viz. the insight that the kingdom is already here); but to those outside all things are obscure' (lit. 'in riddles': *meshalim*, the word underlying *parabolais*, might well bear this meaning since *mashal* sometimes means (e.g. in Ps. 78.2) 'a dark saying').

(d) In v.12 the words after *hina* ('in order that'—expressing God's purpose—'in divine declarations purpose and result are identical') are a free quotation of Isa. 6.9 f., deserving inverted commas.

The Aramaic *dil^ema* underlying *mepote* ('lest') here means 'unless', as the rabbinical exegesis of the passage proves.

Mark, misled by the catchword *parabole*, inserted the saying into his parable-chapter; but, originally, it did not refer to the parables, as it affords no criterion for their interpretation.

This seems to us the best solution.

---

[1] For example, three instances of the 'reverential passive'.

Appendix 2

JESUS AND RABBINIC PARABLES

One of Jülicher's errors was to derive his idea of a parable from Aristotle when he should have gone to the rabbis for its prototype. Thanks to the researches of men like Bugge, Fiebig and Strack-Billerbeck, we now possess numerous rabbinical parables for purposes of comparison.

Three may be quoted which have parallels of one kind or another in the Gospels:

A parable resembling The Two Builders is ascribed to Rabbi Eleazar ben Azariah (c. AD 50-120):

> Whosesoever wisdom is in excess of his works, to what is he like? To a tree whose branches are abundant, and its roots scanty; and the wind comes, and uproots it, and overturns it.
> And whosesoever works are in excess of his wisdom, to what is he like? To a tree whose branches are scanty, and its roots abundant; though all the winds come upon it, they stir it not from its place (*Pirqe Aboth* III, 18).

Like and yet how unlike! Eleazar's parable lacks both the artistry and the tremendous personal claim to be found in Christ's.

Another rabbinical parable[1] affords, at first glance, a close parallel to The Labourers in the Vineyard:

> It is like a king who hired many labourers. But one was outstanding in his work. What did the king do? He took him away and walked to and fro with him. When it was evening, the labourers came to receive their pay, and he gave him, with them, the full amount of his wage. Then the labourers murmured and said, We have worked the whole day, and this man has worked only two hours. Then the king said, This man has done more in two hours than you have done in the whole day.

[1] Strack-Billerbeck, *Kommentar zum Neuen Testament aus Talmud und Midrasch*, IV, 492 f.

So has Rabbi Bun learned more in the Law in twenty-eight years than a clever student could have mastered in a life-time.

Again, how similar—and how different! As St Paul would say, one is a parable of works, the other a parable of grace.

The third, attributed to Rabbi Johanan b. Zakkai (who died about AD 80) reminds us of The Man without the Wedding Garment and The Ten Virgins:

It is like a king who invited his servants to a feast, but he did not fix the time. The wise ones among them arrayed themselves and sat at the entrance to the king's palace. They said, Something is still wanting in the king's palace (i.e. we shall not have long to wait). But the foolish ones among them went on with their ordinary work, saying, Is there ever a feast without long waiting? Suddenly the king called for his servants. The wise among them entered, fitly arrayed as they were. But the foolish ones entered not into his presence, all dirty as they were. Then the king rejoiced over the wise ones, but he was wroth with the foolish ones and said, Let those who arrayed themselves for the feast recline and eat and drink; but let those who did not array themselves for the feast remain standing and watch [1]

It was one of Jülicher's cardinal contentions that a genuine parable of Jesus had only one point of comparison. If it had several such points of likeness, it was on the way to being an allegory and therefore doubtfully authentic.

When we find, however, rabbinical parables which have just such allegorical features, we begin to suspect the soundness of Jülicher's judgment.

Here, for example, is a rabbinical parable[2] which we may call The Man and His Trust. It was used by Rabbi Eleazar to comfort Rabbi Johanan b. Zakkai when he lost his son:

I will tell you a parable. How shall we liken the matter? To a man who received from a king an object for safe keeping. Overwhelmed by a sense of his responsibility, he used to cry every day, O, if only I could get quit of the worry of this trust!

Well, you likewise, master, had a son; he made himself familiar with the Law in all its branches; and then he departed from the world without sin.

[1] P. Fiebig, *Die Gleichnisse Jesu im Lichte der rabb. Gleich.*, 17 f.
[2] S.-B., op. cit., I, 971; Bugge, op. cit., 29.

Should you not then be amenable to comforting, since you have so fortunately restored to God what he entrusted to you?

Here we detect three points of comparison; for obviously the man represents Johanan, the king God, and the trust Johanan's dead son.

The parable of The Fox and the Fishes,[1] attributed to Rabbi Akiba (AD 50-153), is another example of a parable which does not fit Jülicher's Aristotelian strait-jacket:

> Once the evil kingship ordered the Israelites not to busy themselves with the Law. Pappus ben Jehudah met Rabbi Akiba holding an assembly in the street and busying himself with the Law. He said to him, 'Akiba, do you not fear the evil kingship?' Akiba replied, 'I will tell you a parable. What is the matter like? It is like a fox who went along a river bank and saw fishes which gathered together from one place to another. The fox said to them: "Why do you flee away?" They replied, "Because of the nets which men cast over us." He said to them, "If you were minded to mount up on dry land, we might dwell, you and I, as my fathers dwelt with your fathers." They said to him, "Are you he of whom it is said that he is the cleverest of beasts? You are not clever but only rather foolish. If we are already afraid in the place of our life (i.e. in the water), how much more would we be in the place of our death (i.e. on dry land)!"
>
> 'So with us too. If we fear now where we sit and busy ourselves with the Law, in which it is written, "For that is thy life and the length of thy days" (Deut. 30.20), how much more so if we go off and neglect it!'

In this amusing parable not only are several relationships compared, but an explanation is added at the end. Yet, on Jülicher's principles, a true parable should do neither of these things!

Finally, an allegorical parable about a Vineyard and its Tenant may be quoted because the Gospels also contain an allegorical parable about a Vineyard whose genuineness many have doubted on the score of its allegorical character. The speaker is Rabbi Jehuda (AD 155-200):

> The patriarch Rabbi Jehuda spoke a parable. 'With what shall we compare it? With a king who had a vineyard which he gave to

[1] Fiebig, op. cit., 79.

a tenant. The king said to his servants, "Go and gather my vineyard, take my portion and lay the tenant's part in his place." They went at once and obeyed his command. Then the tenant began to weep and cry. The king said to him, "Have I taken anything of yours? Have I not taken what was my own?" He answered, "My Lord, O king, so long as your part was with mine, my part was safe from thief and robber; but now since you have removed your part, see, my part is exposed to robbery and theft." '

The king is the King of all kings, God; the tenant is a man's father and mother; so long as the soul (God's share) is in a man, the man remains safe; but if he dies, he is prey for maggot and worm.[1]

Here is not only an allegory about the soul's relation to God in life and death, but once again an explanation is appended.

Enough has been quoted to show how the rabbis' parables illuminate our Lord's. The rabbis and Jesus often introduce their parables in the same way; they often use a pair of parables; they sometimes devise parables which have several points of likeness. But even more striking are the differences between them. The rabbinical parables often explain Scripture texts; Jesus' parables proclaim the Kingdom of God. Nor can the candid reader fail to note how much more vital, dramatic and compelling are Christ's parables. To compare Jesus as a maker of parables with the rabbis is like comparing Shakespeare with the minor dramatists of his time. In the art of parable he has no peer, and none of the rabbis dare even challenge comparison.

Appendix 3

TWO DISPUTED PARABLES

1. The Wicked Vinedressers[2]

Critics from Jülicher to F. C. Grant have refused this parable to Jesus, declaring it to be an allegory created by the early

[1] S.-B., op. cit., I, 665.   [2] See also Vincent Taylor, St Mark, 472 f.

Church. Their three main objections to its authenticity may be thus summarily stated and answered:

1. It is an open attack on his enemies and therefore historically improbable. Answer: This is precisely what we should expect from One who had just thrown down the gage to his enemies by the cleansing of the Temple.

2. It is an allegorical parable. Answer: If Jesus never used allegory, the objection is final. But not only is Isa. 5.1-7, on which it is based, allegorical, but rabbinical parables (like Akiba's The Fox and the Fishes or that with which Eleazar comforted Johanan on the death of his son) are sometimes strongly allegorical. We may be sure that, if it had suited his purpose, no aesthetic scruples would have prevented Jesus using allegory. Other parables of his certainly contained allegorical elements; and we may well argue that an allegory such as Mark 12 preserves exactly suited his purpose at this climactic point in his ministry.

3. The actions of the vineyard tenants are said to be unnatural (and therefore unhistorical). Answer: On the contrary (as Dodd and Jeremias have shown), in a place and time marked by absentee landlords and agrarian discontent, forcible seizure of ownerless land by desperate men is just what we might expect.

Those who hold it to be an early Christian invention ought to ponder well Burkitt's observation: 'That which is not there in the parable is precisely what some Christian inventor would have put in—some reference to the Resurrection.'

Finally notice that the substance of the parable is to be found in a Q saying (Luke 11.49-51; Matt. 23.34 f.) whose genuineness no sober scholar doubts. If it be replied that this passage makes no reference to the sending of an 'only son' we reply that there is enough evidence to show that at this time 'the Son of God' was a synonym for the Messiah (See Barrett: *St John*, 155).

In short, there is no sound reason for saying that Jesus did not, during his last week in Jerusalem, use all the resources of his imagination to bring home to the Jewish leaders their awful responsibility in rejecting God's Kingdom and Messiah.

2. *The Sheep and the Goats*

Some scholars have doubted the authenticity of this 'parable' arguing that while it may contain genuine logia of Jesus, the whole thing is a Matthean construction.

In a careful linguistic analysis[1] Dr J. A. T. Robinson has detected Matthew's special vocabulary at various points. Thus the opening verse recalls Matt. 16.27 and 19.28. Five times we encounter *tote* 'then' which is a favourite Matthean connective. He further argues that phrases like *the righteous* (meaning 'the elect') and the allusions to *the devil and his angels, the eternal* fire, and *eternal punishment* may well be due to the evangelist. He may be right; but he is on much shakier ground when he makes Matthew responsible for changing *the Son of man* (vs. 31) into *the King* (34-40) since, as Preiss says (op. cit., 47), the moment the Son of man takes his seat on the heavenly throne, he becomes the King Messiah.

On the other hand, we may throw many things into the scale of proof for its authenticity: (1) the closely symmetrical structure which seems to have escaped serious distortion in transmission; (2) the presence of Aramaisms (like *poiein* meaning 'serve', the superfluous Aramaic demonstrative underlying *these* (40,45) and *synagein* with the sense of the Aramaic *kenas* which means (a) 'gather' and (b) 'entertain'. Cf. II Sam. 11.27); (3) the sublime *logia* in vss. 35, 40 which surely have all the marks of genuineness; and (4) the startling features of the whole parable which are difficult to ascribe to any one but Jesus.

Our verdict must therefore be that, despite evidences of Matthean stylization, the parable is substantially genuine.

[1] *New Testament Studies,* May, 1956.

Appendix 4

CONCLUSIONS TO PARABLES

Attentive readers will have noticed that in printing the text of various parables we have often omitted a final verse which applies the parable in a moralizing or hortatory way. For example, at the close of The Labourers in the Vineyard we have left out v. 16, 'So the last will be the first and the first last.'

Are then these generalizing conclusions (as they have been called) not authentic words of Jesus? Not necessarily so, but in their present context they are secondary. Often in them we can hear the voice of the Christian preacher or teacher interpreting the parables to his audience and giving them the widest possible application. Since we do the same thing ourselves when preaching the parables today, we cannot be too scornful of the earliest preachers; but in our attempt to get back to the original meaning of the parables it is usually wise to ignore these 'generalizing conclusions'[1] which, as we shall see, sometimes miss the real points of the parables.

Here are ten examples, with comments.

The Watchman (Mark 13.37): 'What I say to you, I say to *all*, Watch.' Comment: This saying, which is missing in Luke 12.35-38, sounds like a phrase from a Christian sermon.

The Labourers in the Vineyard (Matt. 20.16): 'So *the last* will be first and the first last.' Comment: This saying, possibly suggested by the incidental Matt. 20.8b, really misses the point. The parable teaches no lesson about the reversal of rank at the end, since all the labourers receive precisely the same wage.

The Marriage Feast (Matt. 22.14): '*Many* are called, but few are chosen.' Comment: The truth that a few only are saved is taught neither in The Marriage Feast nor in the appended Man without the Wedding Garment.

The Ten Virgins (Matt 25.13): 'Watch therefore, for you

[1] We have italicized the generalizing phrases.

119

know neither the day nor the hour.' Comment: This saying misses the parable's point completely, since in fact all the maidens, wise as well as foolish, fell asleep! It may have come from the parable of The Watchman (Mark 13.35).

The Talents (Matt. 25.29. Cf. Luke 19.26): 'For to *every one* who has will more be given, and he will have abundance; but from him who has not, even what he has will be taken away.' Comment: A floating saying, found also in Mark 4.25; Matt. 13.12; and Luke 8.18. In its present context it tears apart vv. 28 and 30.

The Rich Fool (Luke 12.21): 'So is he who lays up treasure for himself and is not rich toward God.' Comment: This saying moralizes the parable, blunting the sharp edge of its eschatological warning.

The Servant in Authority (Luke 12.48b): '*Every one* to whom much is given, of him much will be required; and of him to whom men commit much they will demand the more.' Comment: The parable deals with a misused trust, but the saying teaches that the greater the divine gift to a man is, the greater is his responsibility.

Tower Builder and Warring King (Luke 14.33): 'So therefore *whoever* of you does not renounce all that he has, cannot be my disciple.' Comment: The two parables summon to self-examination, the logion to self-denial: two different things.

The Unjust Steward (Luke 16.10): 'He who is faithful in a very little is faithful also in much; and he who is dishonest in a very little is dishonest also in much.' Comment: The parable calls for resourcefulness in a crisis, the saying for faithfulness in unimportant things.

The Pharisee and the Publican (Luke 18.14b): 'For *every one* who exalts himself will be humbled; and he who humbles himself will be exalted.' Comment: The point of the parable is justification before God rather than humiliation and exaltation.

On the whole subject see Jeremias, op. cit., 103-114.

LIST OF PARABLES, WITH INDEX

121

M

City on Hill (Matt. 5.14), 73

Tares (Matt. 13.24-30), 19, 33 f., 45 f., 50

Hid Treasure (Matt. 13.44), 24, 64 f.

Costly Pearl (Matt. 13.45 f.), 35, 64 f.

Dragnet (Matt. 13.47 f.), 19, 46, 50

Householder (Matt. 13.52), 65 f.

Lost Sheep (Matt. 18.12-14), 18, 59 f.

Unmerciful Servant (Matt. 18.23-35), 70 f.

Labourers in Vineyard (Matt. 20. 1-16), 7, 19, 24 f., 29, 52 ff., 98

Two Sons (Matt. 21.28-31), 54 f.

Marriage Feast (Matt. 22.1-10), 23, 27, 55 f., 121

Wedding Garment (Matt. 22.11-13), 19, 56, 116

Ten Virgins (Matt. 25.1-13), 18 f., 23, 85 ff., 121 f.

Talents (Matt. 25.14-30), 12, 79 f., 106 ff., 122

Sheep and Goats (Matt. 25.31-46), 88 ff, 120

L

Physician, heal thyself (Luke 4. 23), 9

Two Debtors (Luke 7.41 ff.), 55

Good Samaritan (Luke 10.30-37), 25 f., 30, 34, 72 f.

Friend at Midnight (Luke 11.5-8), 68 f.

Rich Fool (Luke 12.16-21), 77 f., 122

Barren Figtree (Luke 13.6-9), 26, 82

Places at Table (Luke 14.7-11), 57 f.

Tower-builder (Luke 14.28-30), 65, 122

Warring King (Luke 14.31 f.), 65, 122

Lost Sheep (Luke 15.3-7), 18, 59 f.

Lost Coin (Luke 15.8-10), 10, 37, 60

Prodigal Son (Luke 15.11-32), 14, 15, 24, 29, 60 ff., 92, 108

Unjust Steward (Luke 16.1-8), 33, 67 f., 104 ff., 122

Dives and Lazarus (Luke 16.19-31), 83 f.

Farmer and His Man (Luke 17.7-10), 34, 66

Importunate Widow (Luke 18.1-8), 16, 69 f.

Pharisee and Publican (Luke 18. 10-14), 19, 59, 92 f., 102 f., 122

Pounds (Luke 19.12-27), 19, 79 f.

The total number is 68; but since 8 of these occur in more than one source, the final count is 60.

INDEX OF AUTHORS

INDEX OF SUBJECTS